FORWARD/COMMENTARY

The National Institute of Standards and Technology (NIST) is a measurement standards laboratory, and a non-regulatory agency of the United States Department of Commerce. Its mission is to promote innovation and industrial competitiveness. Founded in 1901, as the National Bureau of Standards, NIST was formed with the mandate to provide standard weights and measures, and to serve as the national physical laboratory for the United States. With a world-class measurement and testing laboratory encompassing a wide range of areas of computer science, mathematics, statistics, and systems engineering, NIST's cybersecurity program supports its overall mission to promote U.S. innovation and industrial competitiveness by advancing measurement science, standards, and related technology through research and development in ways that enhance economic security and improve our quality of life.

The need for cybersecurity standards and best practices that address interoperability, usability and privacy has been shown to be critical for the nation. NIST's cybersecurity programs seek to enable greater development and application of practical, innovative security technologies and methodologies that enhance the country's ability to address current and future computer and information security challenges.

The cybersecurity publications produced by NIST cover a wide range of cybersecurity concepts that are carefully designed to work together to produce a holistic approach to cybersecurity primarily for government agencies and constitute the best practices used by industry. This holistic strategy to cybersecurity covers the gamut of security subjects from development of secure encryption standards for communication and storage of information while at rest to how best to recover from a cyber-attack.

Why buy a book you can download for free?　　We print this so you don't have to.

Some are available only in electronic media. Some online docs are missing pages or barely legible.

We at 4th Watch Publishing are former government employees, so we know how government employees actually use the standards. When a new standard is released, an engineer prints it out, punches holes and puts it in a 3-ring binder. While this is not a big deal for a 5 or 10-page document, many NIST documents are over 100 pages and printing a large document is a time-consuming effort. So, an engineer that's paid $75 an hour is spending hours simply printing out the tools needed to do the job. That's time that could be better spent doing engineering. We publish these documents so engineers can focus on what they were hired to do – engineering. It's much more cost-effective to just order the latest version from Amazon.com

If there is a standard you would like published, let us know. Our web site is: usgovpub.com

NISTIR 8179

Criticality Analysis Process Model

Prioritizing Systems and Components

Celia Paulsen
Jon Boyens
Nadya Bartol
Kris Winkler

This publication is available free of charge from:
https://doi.org/10.6028/NIST.IR.8179

National Institute of
Standards and Technology
U.S. Department of Commerce

NISTIR 8179

Criticality Analysis Process Model

Prioritizing Systems and Components

Celia Paulsen
John Boyens
Computer Security Division
Information Technology Laboratory

Nadya Bartol
Boston Consulting Group
Bethesda, MD

Kris Winkler
Boston Consulting Group
Denver, CO

This publication is available free of charge from:
https://doi.org/10.6028/NIST.IR.8179

April 2018

U.S. Department of Commerce
Wilbur L. Ross, Jr., Secretary

National Institute of Standards and Technology
Walter Copan, NIST Director and Under Secretary of Commerce for Standards and Technology

National Institute of Standards and Technology Internal Report 8179
94 pages (April 2018)

This publication is available free of charge from:
https://doi.org/10.6028/NIST.IR.8179

Comments on this publication may be submitted to:

National Institute of Standards and Technology
Attn: Computer Security Division, Information Technology Laboratory
100 Bureau Drive (Mail Stop 8930) Gaithersburg, MD 20899-8930
Email: scrm-nist@nist.gov

All comments are subject to release under the Freedom of Information Act (FOIA).

Reports on Computer Systems Technology

The Information Technology Laboratory (ITL) at the National Institute of Standards and Technology (NIST) promotes the U.S. economy and public welfare by providing technical leadership for the Nation's measurement and standards infrastructure. ITL develops tests, test methods, reference data, proof of concept implementations, and technical analyses to advance the development and productive use of information technology. ITL's responsibilities include the development of management, administrative, technical, and physical standards and guidelines for the cost-effective security and privacy of other than national security-related information in federal information systems.

Abstract

In the modern world, where complex systems and systems-of-systems are integral to the functioning of society and businesses, it is increasingly important to be able to understand and manage risks that these systems and components may present to the missions that they support. However, in the world of finite resources, it is not possible to apply equal protection to all assets. This publication describes a comprehensive Criticality Analysis Process Model – a structured method of prioritizing programs, systems, and components based on their importance to the goals of an organization and the impact that their inadequate operation or loss may present to those goals. A criticality analysis can help organizations identify and better understand the systems, subsystems, components, and subcomponents that are most essential to their operations and the environment in which they operate. That understanding facilitates better decision making related to the management of an organization's information assets, including information security and privacy risk management, project management, acquisition, maintenance, and upgrade decisions. The Model is structured to logically follow how organizations design and implement projects and systems, can be used as a component of a holistic and comprehensive risk management approach that considers all risks, and can be used with a variety of risk management standards and guidelines.

Keywords

Baseline criticality; criticality; criticality analysis; critical components; critical programs; critical systems; information security; prioritizing components; prioritizing programs; prioritizing systems; prioritization; privacy.

Supplemental Content

An image file of the Criticality Analysis Process Model is available at:
https://csrc.nist.gov/publications/detail/nistir/8179/final

Acknowledgments

The authors, Jon Boyens, National Institute of Standards and Technology (NIST), Celia Paulsen (NIST), Nadya Bartol (Boston Consulting Group), and Kristina Winkler (Boston Consulting Group) would like to acknowledge and thank a number of individuals who provided valuable insights and helped to improve this publication. We would especially like to thank Kelley Dempsey (NIST), Victoria Pillitteri (NIST), Dr. Ron Ross (NIST), Maureen Moore (NIST), Paul Black (NIST), Elizabeth Lennon (NIST), Dr. Carol Woody (SEI CERT), and John Peterson (Redhorse Corporation) for their contribution to the content during the document development and review.

Note to Readers

This document is meant to help its users prioritize critical programs, systems, and components. It is not meant as a stand-alone process, rather it is meant to integrate into already existing processes, such as risk management, information security, security engineering, system and software engineering, privacy engineering, safety, quality, and other related disciplines. The model as described represents an idealized process and may not match every organization's existing processes; readers are encouraged to adapt and integrate the process model described in this publication in a way that best fits the needs and current operations of their organization(s).

Executive Summary

NISTIR 8179 describes a Criticality Analysis Process Model – a structured method of prioritizing programs, systems, and components based on their importance to the mission and the risk that their ineffective or unsatisfactory operation or loss may present to the mission. The Criticality Analysis Process Model presented in this document adopts and adapts concepts presented in risk management, system engineering, software engineering, security engineering, privacy engineering, safety applications, business analysis, systems analysis, acquisition guidance, and cyber supply chain risk management publications.

The Criticality Analysis Process Model can be used as a component of a holistic and comprehensive risk management approach that considers all risks, including information security and privacy risks. The Model can be used with a variety of risk management standards and guidelines including the International Organization for Standardization/International Electrotechnical Commission (ISO/IEC) 27000 family of standards and the suite of National Institute of Standards and Technology (NIST) Special Publications (SPs). The Model can also be used with systems and software engineering frameworks.

The need for criticality analysis within information security emerged as systems have become more complex and supply chains used to create software, hardware, and services have become extended, geographically distributed, and vast. The first mention of criticality analysis in NIST publications is in NIST SP 800-53 Revision 4 (Rev 4), *Security and Privacy Controls for Federal Information Systems and Organizations*. Today, criticality analysis is referenced in several NIST special publications including those addressing risk management, system security engineering, and supply chain risk management.

The Model references and uses the outputs and artifacts of risk management, information security, project management, system design, safety, privacy, and other activities that an organization may already be performing. To reduce potential redundancy and duplication, the Model identifies integration points with these existing processes.

The Criticality Analysis Process Model is structured to logically follow how organizations design and implement projects and systems and can be adapted to fit organizations' unique practices.

The Model consists of five main processes:

A. Define Criticality Analysis Procedure(s) where the organization develops or adopts a set of procedures for performing a criticality analysis.
B. Conduct Program-Level Criticality Analysis where the program manager defines, reviews, and analyzes the program to identify key activities that are vital to reaching the objectives of the program and for reaching the overall goals of the organization.
C. Conduct System/Subsystem-Level Criticality Analysis where the system designer reviews and analyzes the system or subsystem from the point of view of its criticality to the overall organizational goals.
D. Conduct Component/Subcomponent-Level Criticality Analysis where the system or component engineer reviews and analyzes component or subcomponent from the point of

view of its criticality to a specific system or subsystem of which these components and subcomponents are a part.

E. Conduct Detailed Review of Criticality for Processes B, C, and D where the program manager or a collaborative group analyzes baseline criticality analysis results to create final criticality levels for Systems/Subsystems and Components/Subcomponents.

Using this Criticality Analysis Process Model can help organizations to better understand the systems, subsystems, components, and subcomponents that are most essential to their operations. Having this information will facilitate holistic information security and privacy risk management and integration of security and privacy considerations into project management and acquisition. The Model can help increase robustness and granularity of the decisions made about levels of protection afforded to systems and components during system development and acquisition life cycles. It also provides a means for communicating and coordinating priorities with product and service providers.

Table of Contents

List of Appendices

List of Figures

1   Introduction

In the modern world, where complex systems and systems-of-systems are integral to the functioning of society and businesses, it is increasingly important to be able to understand and manage risks that these systems and components may present to the missions that they support. And in the world of finite resources, it is not possible to apply equal protection to all assets. Managing risk can be improved with processes, methods, and techniques to prioritize assets for a detailed risk analysis and for applying information security and privacy controls. However, existing standards and guidelines provide only high-level and fragmented guidance for how to prioritize systems and components in relation to the goals of the organization, the mission, and the environment. Additionally, these existing standards and guidelines are most often focused on prioritizing projects according to organizational goals, or prioritizing components according to system functionality, which can result in an incomplete understanding of the potentially critical nature of a component to organizational goals.

This publication describes a comprehensive Criticality Analysis Process Model (hereafter referred to as "the Model") – a structured method of prioritizing programs, systems, and components based on their importance to the goals of an organization and the impact that their inadequate operation or loss may present to those goals. The Model adopts and adapts concepts presented in risk management, system engineering, software engineering, security engineering, privacy engineering, safety applications, business analysis, systems analysis, acquisition guidance, and cyber supply chain risk management publications. It helps organizations to identify and prioritize information systems and components that are vital to the success of organizational goals.

A criticality analysis is especially pertinent in the current technology environment where organizations rely on third-party product and service providers for the development, integration, and management of the information technology (IT) and operational technology (OT) they use.[1] A criticality analysis can help organizations identify and better understand the systems, subsystems, components, and subcomponents that are most essential to their operations and the environment in which they operate. That understanding facilitates better decision making related to the management of an organization's assets, including information security and privacy risk management, project management, acquisition, maintenance, and upgrade decisions.

1.1   Purpose and Scope

The Criticality Analysis Process Model is intended to be used as a component of a holistic and comprehensive risk management approach that considers all risks, including information security and privacy risks, to prioritize and tailor controls to those risks. The Model can be used with a variety of risk management standards and guidelines including the International Organization for Standardization/International Electrotechnical Commission (ISO/IEC) 27000 family of standards and

---

[1] Operational technology: programmable systems or devices that interact with the physical environment (or manage devices that interact with the physical environment). These systems/devices detect or cause a direct change through the monitoring and/or control of devices, processes, and events. Examples include industrial control systems, building management systems, fire control systems, and physical access control mechanisms.

the suite of National Institute of Standards and Technology (NIST) Special Publications (SPs). It can also be used in conjunction with systems and software engineering, project management, and auditing/attestation frameworks.

The Model can help increase robustness and granularity of the decisions made about levels of protection afforded to systems and components during system development and acquisition life cycles. It also provides a means for communicating and coordinating priorities with product and service providers.

The Model uses existing artifacts, processes, and methods to a maximum extent. It references and uses the outputs of risk management, information security, privacy, project management, system design, safety, and other processes that an organization is already performing. The Model is not intended to replace any of these processes. Rather, to reduce potential redundancy and leverage existing efforts, the Model identifies integration points with these existing processes. An organization may have additional processes not listed in this publication, which may also be performed alongside and integrated with the Model.

1.2 Background

The notion of a formal criticality analysis originated from Failure Mode Effects and Criticality Analysis (FMECA), used in safety applications. The need for a criticality analysis within information security emerged as technology became more complex and supply chains used to create software, hardware, and services became extended, geographically distributed, and vast. The first mention of criticality analysis in NIST publications was in NIST SP 800-53 Revision 4 (Rev. 4), *Security and Privacy Controls for Federal Information Systems and Organizations*. Today, it is mentioned in several NIST special publications including those addressing risk management, system security engineering, and supply chain risk management.

These documents provide high-level guidance on criticality analysis, including how to integrate it into broader risk management, system engineering, or security or privacy engineering activities. However, these publications do not provide detailed guidance for how to perform the criticality analysis itself. A number of U.S. government agencies have implemented criticality analysis processes, but these processes are nonstandard and are often not formally defined. Meanwhile, the need for detailed information for how to identify what is critical and how to prioritize its protection within a system has become more acute due to how modern systems and components are designed, developed, manufactured, acquired, and deployed.

Identifying the asset of greatest importance is not a new concept. A number of disciplines have well-established methods for doing so, including business risk management, project management, safety, supply chain management, supply chain risk management, critical infrastructure protection, and others. These concepts are used in a variety of industries including banking and electric utilities. The authors researched and compared these existing methods and approaches to develop the Model described in this publication; it is anchored in these existing methods and approaches and is tailored specifically to the needs of information security and privacy risk management.

1.3 Audience

The audience for this publication is a broad set of leaders and practitioners including those engaged in cybersecurity/information security; privacy; information technology; contracting; procurement/acquisitions; system and software development/engineering; security engineering; auditors; program management; and system owners. Other personnel or entities are free to use the guidance as appropriate to their situation.

1.4 Relationship to other standards and NIST publications

The Model can be integrated into a variety of processes including information security, risk and privacy management, system and software engineering, acquisition, auditing/attestation, and project management. It can also be used in conjunction with safety, privacy, and business analysis processes. This publication builds on a set of multidisciplinary publications, standards, and guidelines, developed by NIST, the International Organization for Standardization (ISO), and other bodies. "Criticality Analysis" is mentioned in and can be used with the following NIST SPs:[2]

- NIST SP 800-53 Rev. 4, *Security and Privacy Controls for Federal Information Systems and Organizations,* which describes security control SA-14: *Criticality Analysis.*
- NIST SP 800-160 Volume 1, *Systems Security Engineering: Considerations for a Multidisciplinary Approach in the Engineering of Trustworthy Secure Systems,* mentions criticality analysis a part of performing control SA-2: *Perform the security aspects of systems analyses*, as well as in Appendix G: *Engineering and Security Fundamentals.*
- NIST SP 800-161, *Supply Chain Risk Management Practices for Federal Information Systems and Organizations,* mentions the concept of criticality several times:
  - "Baseline Criticality" is mentioned in Task 1-1 to be determined as a part of the Frame step of the Risk Management Process;
  - In Task 2-0, *Criticality Analysis,* a task is to be performed at the beginning of the Assess step in the Risk Management Process, and
  - In the supplemental guidance for control SA-14: *Criticality Analysis.*

Through the above publications, criticality analysis is associated with, and integrated into, the broader set of related NIST publications, including:

- Federal Information Processing Standard Publication (FIPS) 199, *Standards for Security Categorization of Federal Information and Information Systems;*
- NIST SP 800-39, *Managing Information Security Risk: Organization, Mission, and Information System View*, and
- NIST SP 800-30 Rev. 1, *Guide for Conducting Risk Assessments.*

---

[2] Criticality analysis is a fundamental aspect or risk management and is expected to be included in all future versions of the listed publications.

The Criticality Analysis Process Model presented in this document can be used in conjunction with ISO standards focused on risk management or information security in supplier relationships:

- ISO/IEC 27036 – *Information technology – Security techniques – Information security for supplier relationships,*
- ISO/IEC 27001 – *Information technology – Security techniques – Information security management system,*
- ISO/IEC 27002 – *Information technology – Security techniques – Code of practice for information security management,* and
- ISO/IEC 20243 - *Information technology – Open Trusted Technology Provider Standard (O-TTPS) -- Mitigating maliciously tainted and counterfeit products.*

The Criticality Analysis Process Model can also be used in conjunction with additional standards and publications focused on system and software engineering:

- NIST SP 800-160 Volume 1, *Systems Security Engineering,* and
- ISO/IEC/IEEE 15288 – *System and software lifecycle processes International Council on Systems Engineering (INCOSE) System Engineering Handbook.*

1.5   Structure of this document

The rest of this publication is organized as follows:
- Chapter 2 provides an overview of the Model including the methodology used to develop it and tips for how to read the Model diagram itself.
- Chapter 3 provides a deep-dive description of the Model and the processes that compose the Model.
- Appendix A lists acronyms and abbreviations used in this document.
- Appendix B provides the bibliography of sources and references used in this document.
- Appendix C provides a brief overview of methods mentioned in the Model.
- Appendix D provides two illustrative examples of how the Model can be used.
- Appendix E provides a detailed diagram of the Model.

2   Criticality Analysis Process Model Overview

This chapter provides an overview of the Criticality Analysis Process Model including:

- The methodology that was used to develop the Model;
- Overview of the top-level processes in the Model; and
- Guidance on how to read the process diagrams used to depict the Model, including any "rules" for interpreting those diagrams.

2.1   Methodology

The Model was developed by conducting four main activities:

- Environmental scan that included identification and detailed review of publications (listed in Appendix B) from different subject areas that describe methods for identifying critical assets.
- Comparative analysis and synthesis of the reviewed methodologies to derive a common set of steps for a criticality analysis.
- Identification of steps relevant to information security and privacy and potential steps not described in existing literature.
- Translation and transformation of the steps into the information security and privacy practitioner language.

First, the authors identified and collected a number of methodologies that described a process for identifying or prioritizing critical assets. A subset of methodologies was then selected for further research, based on an initial assessment of their potential applicability to an information security and privacy criticality analysis, their comprehensiveness, uniqueness, and usability by the intended audience. The authors also contacted a small number of subject matter experts to provide insights into the various methodologies and those methodologies' usefulness to an information security and privacy criticality analysis.

The authors then summarized and conducted a detailed review of each methodology using a structured matrix format. The summaries included but were not limited to the following information:

- Applicability to an information security and privacy criticality analysis for projects, systems, and components;
- Scalability to large and small projects/organizations;
- Investment/cost considerations;
- Applicability to an existing or new system;
- Inputs and outputs;
- Complexity and difficulty of use; and
- Demonstrated effectiveness in their respective domains.

Next, the authors conducted a comparative analysis and synthesis of the methodologies using another matrix to derive a common set of steps. In addition, additional steps were described that filled gaps related to the application of existing literature to an information security and privacy domain. Once the authors were satisfied with the accuracy and completeness of the comparative analysis, they validated the Model against relevant information security and privacy sources to ensure that the terminology in and the general flow of the Model was consistent with information security and privacy concepts and guidance. Next, the Model itself was constructed using commonly accepted process modeling techniques. The finalized set of steps were translated and transformed into information security and privacy practitioner language and aligned with existing NIST publications. The Model was then edited and simplified for ease of use.

2.2 Model Overview

The Criticality Analysis Process Model is structured to logically follow how organizations design, acquire, and implement projects and systems. Traditionally, organizations establish projects and programs to accomplish mission and business objectives and to guide the performance of corresponding activities. They design and/or deploy information systems to support those activities. These systems are often a loosely defined, complex mixture of hardware, software, network infrastructure, data, humans, and other elements, and may be composed of numerous subsystems (this architecture is often called "systems of systems"). The IT/OT components and subcomponents used to construct these systems and subsystems typically come from a variety of sources and are often Commercial-off-the-Shelf (COTS) products. Different organizational units – including third parties – naturally have different roles and responsibilities with respect to these projects, systems, and components.

The structure of the Model defined in this document accommodates these dynamics and at the same time, helps to facilitate a holistic view of criticality for a collection of programs, systems/subsystems, and components/subcomponents.[3] The Model combines top-down and bottom-up analysis approaches. The top-down approach in this model enables the organization to identify critical processes and then to progressively narrow the analysis to critical systems that support those processes, and then to critical components which ensure the critical functions of those systems. It follows an ideal system development process while allowing the flexibility for analyzing systems and components in a less ideal situation. The bottom-up approach progressively traces the impact of a malfunctioning or compromised critical component would have on the system, and then on the program. It allows for the identification of interactions, intersections, connections, and dependencies between components, systems, and programs that are not easily identified in a top-down approach. The combination of using top-down and bottom-up approaches ensures that the Model is thorough and complete.

The Model consists of five main processes as depicted in Figure 1:

    A. Define Criticality Analysis Procedure
    B. Conduct Program-Level Criticality Analysis
    C. Conduct System/Subsystem-Level Criticality Analysis

---

[3] The model does not require organizations to use standard or identical definitions of program, system, subsystem, component, or subcomponent to allow organizations the flexibility of using their existing definitions; however, the model was developed with the assumption that the systems and components evaluated would be technological in nature (IT/OT). This is explained further in the Model itself.

D. Conduct Component/Subcomponent-Level Criticality Analysis
E. Conduct Detailed Review of Criticality for Processes B, C, and D.

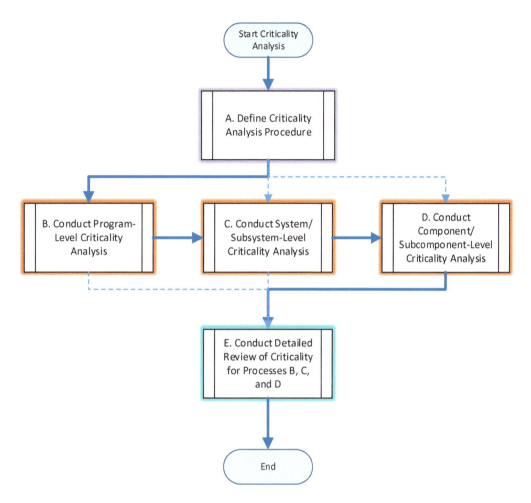

Figure 1 – High-Level Criticality Analysis Process Model

Process A is expected to be completed before other processes. Processes B, C, and D ideally will be performed in sequence to provide a comprehensive top-down analysis, but may be performed at the same time or out of sequence (this is shown in the model with dotted lines). Different individuals typically perform these processes; process D in particular is likely to be done partially by a third party in the case of, for example, COTS products. These three processes have iterative sub-processes and can be conducted at increasing levels of detail to refine the results and accept additional inputs. Process E is a bottom-up analysis using inputs from, and cutting across, processes B, C, and D. It is performed at the very end to finalize criticality levels for programs, systems/subsystems, and components/subcomponents.

Section 3, Model Process and Sub-Process Descriptions, describes each process and sub-process in detail.

2.3 How to Read the Model

The Criticality Analysis Process Model was developed using formal process modeling techniques and flowchart methods. This ensures maximum flexibility for organizations integrating the model and facilitates the integration of the model into existing software-based tools. Users do not need a thorough understanding of the techniques or methods to use the Model.

The following symbols were used:[4]

	Documents within/external to the enterprise
	Output of a sub-process
	Start/end of process
	Decision point
	Sub-process
	Previous process/sub-process
	Iterative Feedback loop

The Model is intended to be read top-down and left-to-right. Boxes around a series of sub-processes indicate that these sub-processes are iterative and can be performed in a loop until an acceptable output is produced.

Each process has "start" and "end" and accepts inputs both from the Model and from other sources. Each process produces outputs that serve as inputs into subsequent processes within the Model.

> Note: Feedback loops are not included in this model due to the extent of iteration and feedback required. Instead, organizations are encouraged to continuously iterate and update throughout the analysis. This is shown in the model as an "Iterative Feedback Loop box."

---

[4] Adapted from ISO 5807:1985, *Documentation symbols and conventions for data, program and system flowcharts, program network charts and system resources charts.*

3   Model Process and Sub-Process Descriptions

This chapter provides detailed descriptions of the Model's processes and sub-processes. The five processes of the Criticality Analysis Process Model are depicted in Figure 1 in Section 2, and a more detailed version of the Model may be found in Appendix E. Each process consists of one or more sub-processes. Detailed diagrams of each process, including the associated sub-processes, are included in the sections below. Appendix D provides two examples of how the Model can be used and adapted.

The first process, *A. Define Criticality Analysis Procedure,* provides guidance, structure, and continuity for performing a criticality analysis, which is necessary due to the number of different people and groups involved in completing a criticality analysis.

The next three processes, *B. Conduct Program-Level Criticality Analysis, C. Conduct System/Subsystem-Level Criticality Analysis, and D. Conduct Component/Subcomponent-Level Criticality Analysis*, act as a top-down means of mapping and prioritizing activities, associated systems/subsystems, and finally, components/subcomponents of those systems. These three processes are very similar to each other conceptually, but require different methods for completion and are typically done by separate groups of people with differing areas of expertise, thus are described separately. They are iterative and can be conducted at increasing level of detail to refine the results and accept additional inputs. Ideally, these three processes would be be conducted in sequence. However, it is likely that for many use cases, they will be conducted at least partially out of sequence or in parallel to each other.

The last process, *E. Conduct Detailed Review of Criticality for Processes B, C, and D*, is performed after Processes *B*, *C*, and *D* have been completed and cuts across these three processes. This process is performed in a bottom-up manner for tracing dependencies and impact/risk from subcomponents to components, components to subsystems, subsystems to systems, systems to programs, and programs to higher-level programs using the information gathered in the previous three processes. It provides connective tissue between Processes *B*, *C*, and *D*, and ensures that the criticality determination is consistent across all layers of the Model – program, system/subsystem, and component/subcomponent – in terms of considering impacts, dependencies, and risks across the entire program. As such, Process E requires a high level of coordination and collaboration between the actors in those other processes. Baseline Criticality levels assigned in Processes *C* and *D* are finalized in process *E*; the Baseline Criticality levels determined in Process *B* are typically sufficient for the program level and so do not need to be finalized in Process *E*.

Note: Organizations do not need to complete each process or sub-process exactly as described in this document to complete a criticality analysis. Rather, organizations are expected to tailor this Model to their own needs, capabilities, and operating environment.

The sections below describe inputs, outputs, and methods associated with each Process of the Model. These are listed for informational purposes only, and it is expected that users will fill in these items with information specific to their organization(s) when they tailor the Model as described in process A.1. The inputs listed provide examples of the types of documents that may be useful in completing the process/sub-process. Organizations may not have all the inputs mentioned in this publication. If a specific input does not exist or is unavailable for any reason, the same type of information may exist as part of another document or in another format. Similarly, outputs described in this publication do not need to be stand-alone documents but may be part of an existing document or be available in another format than is described herein.

The methods listed are intended to provide additional guidance on how to complete the sub-processes. These methods are briefly described in Appendix C, with references for further guidance where available. In tailoring the Model, it may be useful to more fully describe or provide information on methods to be used.

This chapter describes each process and the associated sub-processes in detail. Each process is described using the following template:

Process	Letter designator of the process
Process name	Name of the process
Process summary	Description of the process
Inputs	Documents that may be useful in completing the process.
Outputs	Documents that are created or modified as a result of completing the process. There are two types of outputs: Informal outputs that capture information passed from a sub-process to the next sub-process. Those outputs may include working documents or emails and are not depicted as outputs in the Model. Outputs that produce formal documentation, although the nature of that documentation is flexible. Each process produces at least one piece of formal documentation that is depicted in the Model.
Roles and Responsibilities	List of roles regarding who will be Responsible, Accountable, Consulted, or Informed of the sub-process and its outputs. Roles may vary according to size and complexity of an organization. Many of the roles listed in this publication are described in more detail in NIST SP 800-181, *National Initiative for Cybersecurity Education (NICE) Cybersecurity Workforce Framework*.
Related processes outside of criticality analysis	A sample list of publications (with link to full citation in Appendix B.2) describing security, privacy, engineering, business, etc., processes that are related to, but not directly included in, criticality analysis. Knowing how these related processes relate to criticality analysis may help identify areas where existing work may be leveraged and provide some context in understanding the criticality analysis process.

Each sub-process will be summarized using the following template:

Sub-process ID	Number designator of the sub-process
Sub-process name	Name of the sub-process
Sub-process description	Description of the sub-process
Inputs	Documents that may be useful in completing the sub-process.
Outputs	Documents that serve as outputs from the sub-process. There are two types of outputs: Informal outputs that capture information passed from a sub-process to the next sub-process. Those outputs may include working documents or emails and are not depicted as outputs in the Model. Outputs that produce formal documentation, although the nature of that documentation is flexible. These outputs are depicted in the Model.
Methods	Methods that may be used in the performance of the sub-process.
Related processes outside of criticality analysis	A sample list of publications (with link to full citation in Appendix B.2) describing security, privacy, engineering, business, or other processes that are related to or tie in with this sub-process, its inputs, or its outputs. Knowing how these related processes relate to the criticality analysis may help identify areas where existing work may be leveraged and provide some context in understanding the criticality analysis process.

3.1 Process A – Define Criticality Analysis Procedure

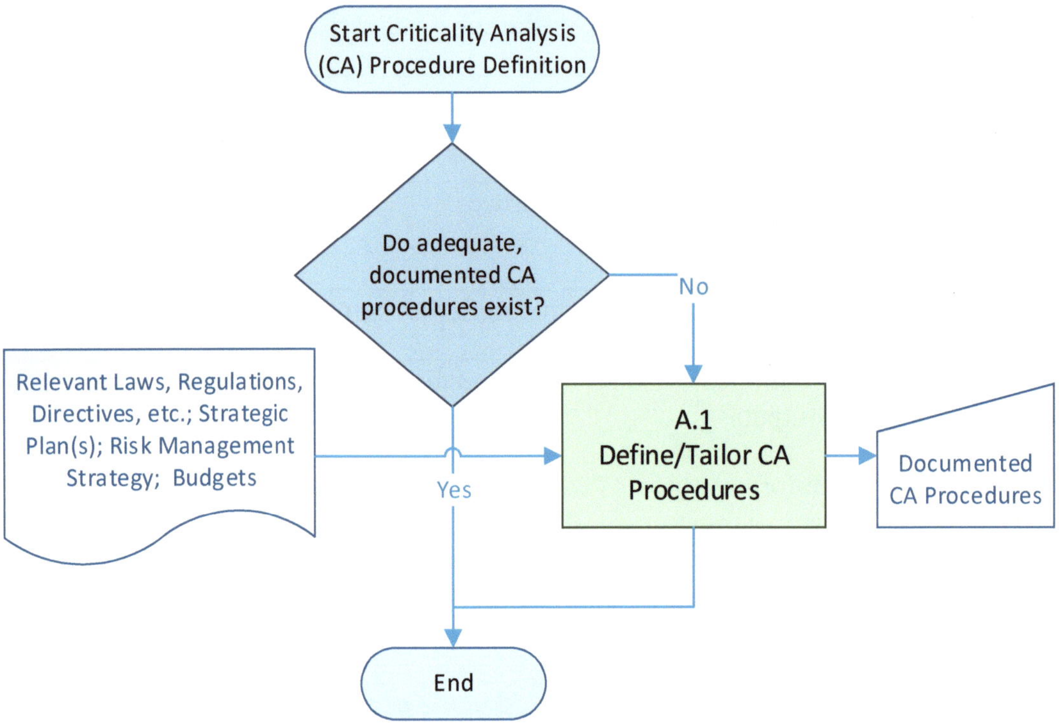

Figure 2 - Define Criticality Analysis Procedure

Process A, *Criticality Analysis Procedure Definition,* depicted in Figure 2, is completed before the rest of the criticality analysis is performed. This process ensures that there is a set of documented procedures to guide the criticality analysis. It helps set up for a successful execution of the criticality analysis by providing scoping, framing, and procedural guidance for conducting a criticality analysis.

Process A consists of the following:

- Check if documented procedures exist and if they are sufficient and appropriate for the needs of the criticality analysis;
- If procedures exist, then Process A can end and Process B can begin;
- If procedures do not exist or are not sufficient or appropriate for the needs of the criticality analysis, sub-process A.1, *Define/Taylor Criticality Analysis Procedures,* is performed to develop or tailor procedures for the criticality analysis; and
- Once the procedures have been satisfactorily defined or tailored in sub-process A.1, Process A can end and Process B can begin.

The output of this process is "Documented Criticality Analysis Procedures." The intent of this process is to ensure there is a document that provides guidance on how to conduct a criticality analysis; a document named "Criticality Analysis Procedure" is not necessary. A project plan, program plan, program implementation plan, or other kind of plan may provide sufficient guidance.

Process number	A
Process name	Criticality Analysis Procedure Definition
Process summary	The organization either develops procedures that would guide the criticality analysis, or, if such procedures exist, finds them and, if needed, tailors them to the specific needs of the program.
Inputs	None
Outputs	Documented Criticality Analysis Procedures
Responsible persons	Responsible: Project Manager in charge of the criticality analysis Accountable: Program Manager can delegate the execution of this process to a Business Analyst or other suitable individual. Consulted: Individuals who understand the organizations' operational environment; individuals with project management, process management, or criticality analysis experience; individuals who developed the criticality analysis model being tailored. Informed: Individuals responsible for conducting any part of the criticality analysis.
Related processes outside of criticality analysis	[NIST SP 800-39] – (3.1) Framing Risk [NIST SP 800-160] – (3.3.1) Project Planning Process [NIST SP 800-161] – (2.2.1) Frame

A.1 – Define/Tailor Criticality Analysis Procedures

Sub-process ID	A.1
Sub-process name	Define/Tailor Criticality Analysis Procedures
Sub-process description	Develop procedures for conducting a criticality analysis by adapting this Model to the organization's structure, environment, and existing processes. If a criticality analysis procedure has already been adapted by an organization, tailor or refine that procedure to the needs and environment of the specific criticality analysis being conducted. The criticality analysis procedure:

	defines the scope, describes any assumptions to be made, identifies responsible parties, and details the procedures to be used in conducting the analysis. It may be tailored to, for example, existing procedures which supersede or align closely with procedures in the model, define how specific sub-processes are to be completed, or rearrange the sub-processes to better fit organizational processes. Because the criticality analysis will likely be performed by multiple groups and individuals, ensure that the proceedure definition includes requirements as to how the groups and individuals are to communicate. Include requirements for any documents that may be transferred between individuals; ensure those individuals have appropriate permissions to review the information in those documents. Include in the procedure what events or conditions (i.e., triggers) result in the need for a criticality analysis. Some organizations may also define the events or conditions (i.e., triggers) that will launch each stage(s) of the analysis. Describe what events or conditions (i.e., triggers) necessitate a full or partial review/update of existing criticality analysis, and how those events or conditions will be monitored for and reported. For example, a review/update may be needed if a new vulnerability is discovered, the environment of operation changes, or a modification to a portion of the system is proposed. Some organizations may choose to regularly review their criticality analyses. Carefully review the scope and purpose of the review. When defining roles and responsibilities, include individuals responsible for, accountable for, consulted on, or informed about each process and sub-process in this Model. Define how and when these individuals will communicate. This is especially important in cases where different organizational units or third parties will be conducting portions of the analysis. Consider any relevant contractual requirements.
Inputs	Relevant Laws, Regulations, Directives, etc.; Strategic Plan(s); Risk Management Strategy; Budgets
Outputs	Documented Criticality Analysis Procedures
Methods	Project Planning; Document Review
Related processes outside of	[NIST SP 800-39] – (3.1) Framing Risk

criticality analysis	[NIST SP 800-160] – (3.3.1) Project Planning Process [NIST SP 800-161] – (2.2.1) Frame

3.2   Process B – Conduct Program-Level Criticality Analysis

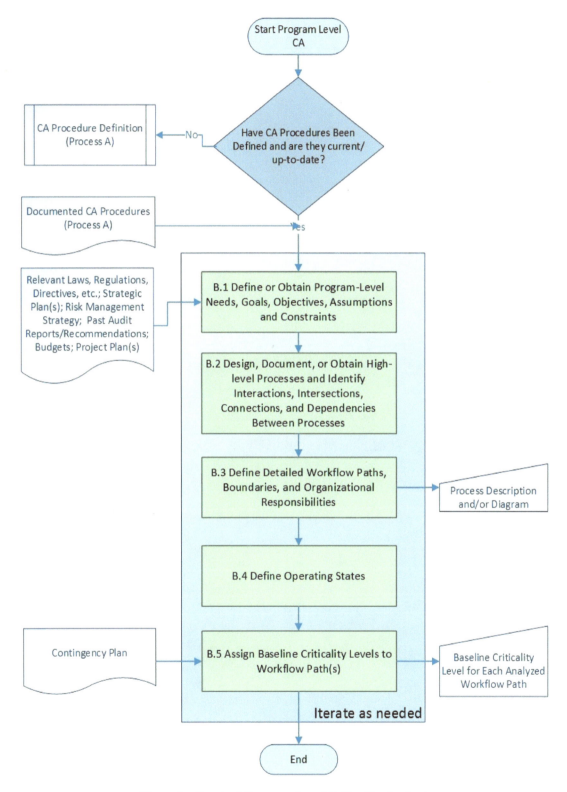

Figure 3 - Conduct Program-Level Criticality Analysis

Process B, *Conduct Program-Level Criticality Analysis*, depicted in Figure 3, is the first layer of the top-down portion of the criticality analysis. It is used to identify and prioritize mission/business objectives, goals, and requirements. While these priorities may be sometimes predefined, at other times, it is through this process that they may be defined or refined. This process is closely tied to Step 1 – Risk Framing described in [NIST SP 800-39] .

For this publication, a program does not necessarily mean an official government program; it may be a collection of programs, an initiative, or an idea. It is defined by a set of mission/business objectives and encompasses the activities that the organization performs to accomplish those objectives. The program may be formally defined in a mission statement, project plan, or other similar document, it may be a concept under development, or it may be a situation that the organization routinely faces but does not fall under any single program's responsibilities. Ideally, Process B would start at the highest level of an organization and repeat iteratively with increasing granularity until the lowest hierarchy of programs is reached. In most cases, this is impractical, and so this Model allows users to begin with any program for which the information required to perform a criticality analysis is available. Appendix D provides examples of how the Model may be used both with an existing, well-defined program and one that is not as well defined.

Process B helps the user define the program and identify key activities that are necessary to ensure that the main goals and objectives of the program are met. It consists of the following:

- Obtain or define program goals and objectives, assumptions, and constraints;
- Obtain, design, or document a high-level process for completing the objectives of the program;
- Identify interactions, intersections, connections, and dependencies within the program process;
- Define how the program will operate normally and and how will it operate if impacted by an adverse operating state (an operating state that is not normal); and
- Assign Baseline Criticality levels to workflow paths based on gathered information.

Much of this process may already be conducted as part of strategic planning or project planning efforts.

Process	B
Process name	Conduct Program-Level Criticality Analysis
Process summary	Define, review, and analyze the program to identify key activities that are vital to reaching the objectives of the program and for reaching the overall goals of the organization. This process ensures that that the criticality determinations for systems/subsystems and components/subcomponents can

	be directly traced back to the objectives of the program and the goals of the organization.
Inputs	Documented Criticality Analysis Procedures (from Process A); Relevant Laws, Regulations, Directives, etc.; Strategic Plan(s); Risk Management Strategy; Past Audit Reports/Recommendations; Budget; Project Plan(s); Contingency Plan
Outputs	Process Description and/or Diagram; Baseline Criticality Levels of Activity(ies) and/or Workflow Path(s)
Roles and Responsibilities	Responsible: Program Manager responsible for the performance of this process. Business Analyst and Lead Security Engineer may serve as a co-lead for sub-processes B.4, Define Operating States, and B5, Assign Baseline Criticality Levels to Workflow Path(s). Accountable: Program Manager can delegate the execution of this process to a Business Analyst or other suitable individual. Consulted: Individuals who have detailed knowledge of the activities identified by this process contribute to the identification of such activities. These individuals may include system architects and designers, system engineers, security or privacy engineers, other security or privacy professionals, acquisition/procurement professionals, business leaders, legal experts/general council, and others, as appropriate. Invite representatives of each relevant group to participate in this process. Informed: Individuals responsible for conducting any part of the criticality analysis.
Related processes outside of criticality analysis	[ISO 21500] [ISO/IEC 22301] [ISO/IEC 27001] [NIST SP 800-34] [NIST SP 800-39] – (3.1) Framing Risk [NIST SP 800-160] – (3.4.1) Business or Mission Analysis Process [NIST SP 800-160] – (3.4.2) Stakeholder Needs and Requirements Definition Process [NIST SP 800-161] – (2.2.1) Frame

B.1 – Define or Obtain Program Level Needs, Goals, Objectives, Assumptions, and Constraints

Sub-process ID	B.1
Sub-process name	Define or Obtain Program-Level Needs, Goals, Objectives, Assumptions and Constraints
Sub-process description	This process helps define the program being analyzed. It lays the foundation for the criticality analysis, establishes context, and provides a common perspective on the assumptions, constraints, risk tolerances, and priorities/trade-offs used for making investment and operational decisions. Define how the success or failure of the program will be measured. Identify a high-level objective or set of related objectives. It is best if there is only one objective or if the set of objectives are closely related to focus the analysis. Measurable goals for the objective(s) are described and include any high-level organizational goals that apply. Consider security, safety, privacy, and other related goals. If there are several objectives and goals, consider their priorities and documenting these priorities. Requirements or constraints are clearly identified and may include applicable legal regulations, organizational policy, risk tolerance, budgets, and any other constraints that may impact the flexibility of the organization's activities. Finally, any assumptions that may impact the analysis are defined. These may include environmental, legal, budgetary, or other variables that may have some degree of uncertainty. An example of an assumption could be "assuming no change in budget," or "assuming an operating environment consistent with typical local weather." Goals, objectives, assumptions, and constraints may be available from current documentation or may need to be developed.
Inputs	Documented Criticality Analysis Procedures (or project plan) from Process A; Relevant Laws, Regulations, Directives (including organizational policies), and other high-level guiding documents that may have the right information; Strategic Plan(s); any documentation that describes organizational mission/vision; needs, goals, objectives, and projects; Risk Management Strategy (including risk tolerance); Budgets and Project Plan(s)
Outputs	Documentation of goals, objectives, assumptions, and constraints
Methods	Project Plan; Document Review; Brainstorming; Process Flow Diagram; Responsible/Accountable/Consulted/Informed (RACI) Charts.

Related processes outside of criticality analysis	[CSF] – (ID.BE-3, 4) Business Environment, (ID.GV-1, 2, 3) Governance [NIST SP 800-39] – (3.1) Framing Risk [NIST SP 800-160] – (3.4.1) Business or Mission Analysis Process [NIST SP 800-160] – (3.4.2) Stakeholder Needs and Requirements Definition Process [NIST SP 800-161] – (2.2.1) Frame

B.2 – Design, Document, or Obtain High-level Processes and Identify Interactions, Intersections, Connections, and Dependencies Between Processes

Sub-process ID	B.2
Sub-process name	Design, Document, or Obtain High-level Processes and Identify Interactions, Intersections, Connections, and Dependencies Between Processes
Sub-process description	This sub-process develops a map, diagram, or other representation of the activities or processes used to accomplish the goals and objectives defined in B.1. Loosely describe the main activities or processes that will be conducted to reach the goals and objectives defined in B.1. Include any activities that will be conducted in a regular course of events to measure the performance of the program, and activities that will be conducted in case of an adverse event (i.e., contingency plans). If possible, identify at a high level all activities regularly conducted by the organization(s) responsible for the completion of the program, including those responsible for performing the identified activities. This may include things such as inspections, maintenance, payroll processing, recruitment/training, or any other activity that may have an impact on the successful completion of the project. Consider identifying triggers that cause an activity to begin and end. Consider defining which activities directly relate to the success of the objective(s), mission(s) or goal(s), and which activities support, but do not directly impact those objective(s), mission(s) or goal(s). Consider identifying conditions or triggers which would cause an activity to be more or less vital or impactful, especially if including activities conducted as part of a contingency plan. Examine interactions between activities or processes and determine which processes rely on the outputs of other processes. Create a map, diagram, or

	other representation of the processes. Ensure that this representation describes connections between the activities or processes, including what processes must be completed before another can begin (e.g., a document created by one process is used in the completion of another). Consider identifying what information or types of information are used by a process or activity. Trace how that information is obtained and how it is used.
Inputs	Documentation of goals, objectives, assumptions, and constraints from B.1.
Outputs	Description of workflow paths, boundaries, and roles and responsibilities to pass to B.3. (This can be done in a document, spreadsheet, or draft process diagram.)
Methods	Graphs with Results and Actions Inter-related (GRAI) Integrated Methodology (GIM); Project Plan; Document Review; Brainstorming; Process Visualization; RACI Charts; Interviews; Observation; Sequence Diagrams; Scenario/Use-Case
Related processes outside of criticality analysis	[CSF] – (ID.AM-3, 6) Asset Management [NIST SP 800-34] [NIST SP 800-39] – (3.1) Framing Risk [NIST SP 800-160] – (3.4.1) Business or Mission Analysis Process [NIST SP 800-160] – (3.4.2) Stakeholder Needs and Requirements Definition Process [NIST SP 800-161] – (2.2.1) Frame

B.3 –Define Detailed Workflow Paths, Boundaries, and Organizational Responsibilities

Sub-process ID	B.3
Sub-process name	Define Detailed Workflow Paths, Boundaries, and Organizational Responsibilities
Sub-process description	This sub-process helps define workflow paths and identify connection points within the program that may be stressed in an adverse situation. Review the representation developed in B.2 and identify closely connected sets of activities to define a workflow. Workflows have an identifiable

<table>
<tr><td></td><td>beginning and end. Consider including in the representation any outputs or products that will be created and transferred between activities.

If the high-level program workflow path is complex or the activities within the workflow are complex, separate the workflow into different processes or workflow paths (also known as "mission threads"). Each workflow path has an identifiable beginning and end. The more detail that is put into this representation, the more specific and tailored the overall criticality analysis can be. However, very detailed diagrams are also less flexible to changes and can be time-consuming to create; it is important to define what level of detail is necessary for the criticality analysis.[5]

Once the activities are identified and represented in a workflow or set of workflow paths, boundaries of those activities are defined and described, and individuals or entities who will be performing those activities identified. Boundaries may be defined in terms of time, triggers, functionalities, systems, organizational units, or any system that makes sense to the user.

The boundaries and responsible individuals are documented in sufficient detail to provide enough information to identify which points in the process may be critical to the organization as analyzed in sub-processes B.4 and B.5, and Process E.

Examine the workflow paths and determine where they intersect and/or depend on each other. Highlight or otherwise clearly identify any activity or output that multiple workflows depend upon.

Consider the boundaries defined in B.2 and identify situations where one activity is dependent on an output or activity located in a different boundary, is outside of the defined workflow path(s), or is outside the scope of the criticality analysis. Consider identifying the amount of control the organization has over certain dependencies (e.g., weather). Also, consider the individuals/responsibilities defined in B.2 and identify where multiple activities are conducted by a single individual or organizational unit. If appropriate, create or update the process diagram or other representation depicting the workflow paths to include interactions, intersections, connections, and dependencies.</td></tr>
<tr><td>**Inputs**</td><td>Description of workflow paths, boundaries, and roles and responsibilities from B.2.</td></tr>
</table>

---

[5] The workflow paths will traverse multiple systems that are supporting the program, which means that there will be handoffs between systems, traversing of system boundaries, transfer between different organizations or individuals, and other events that involve transition.

Outputs	Process Description and/or Diagram; listing of interactions, intersections, connections, and dependencies to pass to B.4.
Methods	Document Review; Process Flow Analysis; GRAI-GIM; Interdependency Analysis; Activity Network Diagram; Gantt Chart; Scenario/Use Case; Mission Thread Analysis; Sensitivity/Uncertainty Analysis.
Related processes outside of criticality analysis	[CSF] – (ID.BE-4) Business Environment [NIST SP 800-39] – (3.1) Framing Risk [NIST SP 800-160] – (3.4.1) Business or Mission Analysis Process [NIST SP 800-160] – (3.4.2) Stakeholder Needs and Requirements Definition Process [NIST SP 800-161] – (2.2.1) Frame

B.4 – Define Operating States

Sub-process ID	B.4
Sub-process name	Define Operating States
Sub-process description	This sub-process describes regular operation of the program and what might happen if the activities or workflow paths defined in B.2 are compromised. For each activity defined in B.2 and B.3, describe the condition of the activity (i.e., what the activity could look like) and the impact on the workflow if the activity is forced into different conditions, including but not limited to: Non-operational (i.e., the activity does not occur); Impaired (i.e., the activity operates at a reduced pace or in an unsafe/insecure/privacy-invasive manner); Normal operation (i.e., how the activity operates under typical or ideal circumstances); Increased operations (i.e., the activity performs quicker or with more output than normal); or Unintended operations (i.e., the activity performs but with additional outputs or actions that are not part of the expected routine).

	Determine the severity of the operating states other than normal (adverse operating states) on the workflow. This could be a ranking (e.g., low, moderate, high) or measure (e.g., time lost; cost in time/resources). Consider defining what types of scenarios would lead to such situations. Examples of scenarios to consider include reduced performance (e.g., lower bandwidth), security breach, privacy problems, physical accident, or any other similar event (often described as an "adverse event" in security and privacy risk assessment models). Consider the time frame of an operating state– often long-term adverse operating states have greater impact than short-term states. Consider how long an adverse operating state must last before it becomes severe. Consider security, safety, and privacy ramifications. Examples of potential ramifications include (but are not limited to): determination of what information is made vulnerable if the activity is performed more slowly than expected, potential physical damages if an activity is performed too quickly, and privacy implications for personally identifiable information if unintended operations are performed. Also consider any contractual, statutory, or other obligations which may be impacted by the operating state. Then, using the Process Description and/or Diagram created in B.3, identify specific interactions, intersections, connections, and dependencies in the workflow paths that would be impacted by each adverse operating state. The purpose is to identify how the adverse operating states of the activity impact other activities in the process and in turn, which interactions or dependencies have the most influence on normal operation of the program and thus are more critical.
Inputs	Process Description and/or Diagram; listing of interactions, intersections, connections, and dependencies from B3.
Outputs	Description of Operating States
Methods	Document Review; Brainstorming; Interviews; Group Decision Making
Related processes outside of criticality analysis	[NIST SP 800-39] – (3.1) Framing Risk [NIST SP 800-160] – (3.4.1) Business or Mission Analysis Process [NIST SP 800-160] – (3.4.2) Stakeholder Needs and Requirements Definition Process

	[NIST SP 800-161] – (2.2.1) Frame

B.5 – Assign Baseline Criticality Levels to Workflow Path(s)

Sub-process ID	B.5
Sub-process name	Assign Baseline Criticality Levels to Workflow Path(s)
Sub-process description	This sub-process determines criticality levels of workflow paths defined in B.3 against operating states defined in B5. Using the Process Description and/or Diagram created in B.2 and B.3, consider how the program would be affected by each of the operating states defined in B.4. Rank the activities, workflow paths, and/or bounded areas according to how vital they are to the success of the objectives/goals defined in B.1 and how strongly an adverse operating state will affect the program objectives and goals. The user creates a way to measure or rank the workflow paths according to how important they are to the success of the program. This could be a ranking (e.g., low, moderate, high), or measure (e.g., time lost; cost in time/resources; probability of being able to complete activity). The user could also use ranges and thresholds to define such rankings.[6] Consider the life cycle of the activities and workflow paths in relation to the project. Considerations may include end dates of activities or workflow paths, and conditions that influence the criticality of activities.
Inputs	Process Description and/or Diagram from B.3; Listing of interactions, intersections, connections, and dependencies from B.3; Listing of operating states from B.4; Contingency Plan
Outputs	Baseline Criticality for each analyzed workflow path.
Methods	Document Review; Group Decision Making
Related processes outside of criticality analysis	[FIPS 199] [NIST SP 800-39] – (3.1) Framing Risk

---

[6] For further guidance on example security measures and metrics, see Appendix A of NIST SP 800-55 Revision 1, *Performance Measurement Guide for Information Security*. Future updates to this publication will also address privacy considerations [NIST SP 800-55].

	[NIST SP 800-160] – (3.4.1) Business or Mission Analysis Process [NIST SP 800-160] – (3.4.2) Stakeholder Needs and Requirements Definition Process [NIST SP 800-161] – (2.2.1) Frame

3.3 Process C– Conduct System/Subsystem-Level Criticality Analysis

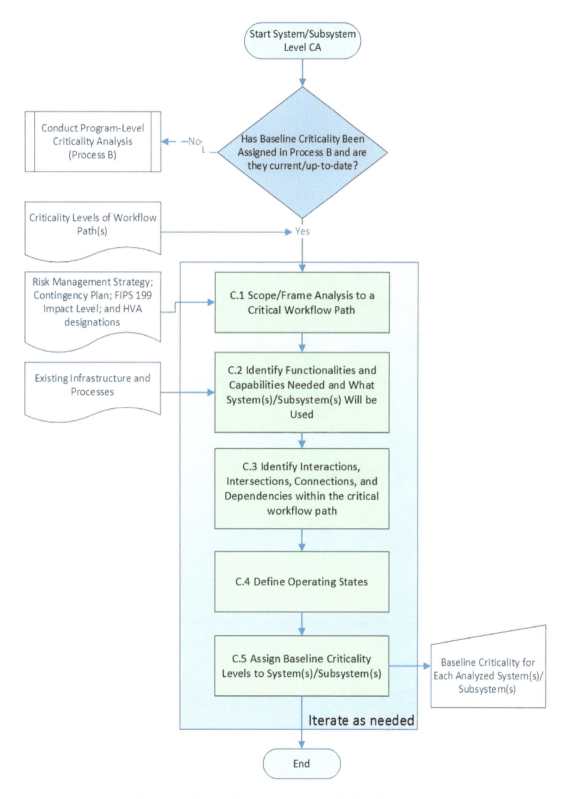

Figure 4 - System/Subsystem-Level Criticality Analysis

Process C, *Conduct System/Subsystem-Level Criticality Analysis,* depicted in Figure 4, is ideally performed after Process B, *Conduct Program-Level Criticality Analysis,* is complete. The process may be repeated at increasingly granular levels to break a complex system down into its smallest parts, until the lowest hierarchical level of subsystem is analyzed. A system or subsystem[7] may include multiple components or subcomponents, often COTS products, each of which may require its own criticality analysis to be performed in Process D. Similarly, one system may support numerous programs; this will be discussed and analyzed in Process E.

Process C consists of the following:

- Scope or frame the analysis to a critical workflow path or paths;
- Identify functionalities/capabilities needed;
- Identify systems/subsystems to be used;
- Define what the system/subsystem will look like when it is operating normally or impacted by an adverse event, that is referred to as an adverse operating state; and
- Assign Baseline Criticality to the workflow paths identified earlier.

Much of this process may be conducted as part of project planning, system design, and acquisition processes.

Process	C
Process name	Conduct System/Subsystem-Level Criticality Analysis
Process summary	This process reviews and analyzes the system or subsystem from the point of view of its criticality to the overall organizational goals.
Inputs	Documented Criticality Analysis Procedures (Process A); Final Criticality Levels of Activity(ies) and/or Workflow Path(s) of Program (Process B); Risk Management Strategy; Contingency Plan; Federal Information Processing Standard (FIPS) 199 Impact Level; High Value Asset (HVA) designations; Existing Infrastructure and Processes

---

[7] System: Any organized assembly of resources and procedures united and regulated by interaction or interdependence to accomplish a set of specific functions. See also information system. (SOURCE: [CNSSI 4009])

Subsystem: A major subdivision or component of an information system consisting of information, information technology, and personnel that perform one or more specific functions. (SOURCE: [NIST SP 800-53]; [NIST SP 800-53A]; [NIST SP 800-37])

System: Combination of interacting elements organized to achieve one or more stated purposes.
Note 1: There are many types of systems. Examples include: general and special-purpose information systems; command, control, and communication systems; crypto modules; central processing unit and graphics processor boards; industrial/process control systems; flight control systems; weapons, targeting, and fire control systems; medical devices and treatment systems; financial, banking, and merchandising transaction systems; and social networking systems.
Note 2: The interacting elements in the definition of system include hardware, software, data, humans, processes, facilities, materials, and naturally occurring physical entities.
Note 3: System of systems is included in the definition of system. (SOURCE: [ISO/IEC/IEEE 15288])

Outputs	Baseline Criticality for Each Analyzed System/Subsystem
Roles and Responsibilities	Responsible: Lead System Architect or a similar role is responsible for the performance of this sub-process. Lead Security Engineer serves as a co-lead for sub-processes C.4, Define Operating States, and C.5, Assign Baseline Criticality Levels to System(s)/Subsystem(s). Accountable: Lead System Architect can delegate the execution of this process to another suitable individual, e.g., Business Analyst or systems analyst. Consulted: Individuals who have detailed knowledge of the activities identified by this process contributes to the identification of critical activities. These individuals may include system architects and designers, system engineers, security or privacy engineers, and other security or privacy professionals, acquisition/procurement professionals, business leaders, legal experts/general counsel, third-party supplier representatives, and others, as appropriate. Invite representatives of each relevant group to participate in this process. Informed: Individuals responsible for conducting any part of the criticality analysis.
Related processes outside of criticality analysis	[ISO/IEC/IEEE 15288] [NIST SP 800-39] – (3.1) Framing Risk [NIST SP 800-160] – (3.4.1) Business or Mission Analysis Process [NIST SP 800-160] – (3.4.2) Stakeholder Needs and Requirements Definition Process [NIST SP 800-161] – (2.2.1) Frame

C.1 – *Scope/Frame Analysis to a Critical Workflow Path*

Sub-process ID	C.1
Sub-process name	Scope/Frame Analysis to Critical Workflow Path
Sub-process description	This sub-process involves identifying which critical process path will be examined further and is necessary for performing a criticality analysis for systems/subsystems. Ideally, it is performed once Baseline Criticality Levels of Activity(ies) and/or Workflow Path(s) have been determined. If

| | criticality levels have not been determined, strongly consider returning to Process B, *Conduct Program-Level Criticality Analysis.*

Use the documentation and Criticality Levels developed in Process B, along with any other relevant laws, policies, directives, etc., to identify which critical activities or workflows are to be further analyzed. If more than one workflow path or set of related activities are determined to be critical in Process B, analyze them separately in Process C unless they are very similar. If there are many activities in one workflow, identify similar types of activities or activities grouped by the boundaries defined in Process B. Ensure that the scope of process C is limited to a set of closely related activities.

If Process B was not completed, if the organization wishes to focus on a certain type of system, or if the organization wishes to focus on a particular function, documents such as the Risk Management Strategy, Contingency Plans, FIPS 199 Impact Level, and High Value Asset (HVA) designations, it may be useful to help identify systems that may be further analyzed to scope the analysis.

Ensure that the scope has definitive boundaries. Define any assumptions or constraints that will help limit the analysis. |
|---|---|
| **Inputs** | Criticality Levels of Activity(ies) and/or Workflow Path(s) from Process B.

Other inputs: Risk Management Strategy; Contingency Plan; FIPS 199 Impact Level; and HVA designations |
| **Outputs** | Scope of analysis to pass to C.2. |
| **Methods** | Document Review; Context Diagram; Decision Analysis |
| **Related processes outside of criticality analysis** | [NIST SP 800-39] – (3.1) Framing Risk

[NIST SP 800-60]

[NIST SP 800-160] – (3.4.1) Business or Mission Analysis Process

[NIST SP 800-160] – (3.4.2) Stakeholder Needs and Requirements Definition Process

[NIST SP 800-161] – (2.2.1) Frame |

C.2 – Identify Functionalities and Capabilities Needed and What System(s)/Subsystem(s) will be Used

Sub-process ID	C.2
Sub-process name	Identify Functionalities and Capabilities Needed and What System(s)/Subsystem(s) Will be Used
Sub-process description	This sub-process defines those functionalities and capabilities that are critical for successful operation of the system/subsystem. Review the activities identified in C.1; list the functionalities and capabilities that are needed to support that activity. Consider what information or type of information is needed for the activity: how it will be processed and secured (covering the full data life cycle[8]). Consider how the activity or related activities are currently conducted and identify any capabilities or tools that are used. Specifically identify functionalities and capabilities that are required by law, regulation, or policy. Also, identify any functionalities that directly support any security, safety, privacy, or similar goals. Consider identifying the frequency of use of functions and capabilities and describing end-of-life conditions such as when the functions/capabilities are expected to no longer be needed, in respect to the workflow or project. Determine whether there is available existing infrastructure sufficient to support the functions and capabilities described in C.2. Identify any functions or capabilities that are not supported by existing infrastructure. Determine what (if any) functions or capabilities will be supported by new systems/subsystems. Consider selecting a range of systems/subsystems that meet the functions and capabilities needed for the program, and rank them according to systems/subsystems that best provide the functions and capabilities noted as necessary.
Inputs	Scope from C.1; Existing Infrastructure and Processes; Existing Contractual Obligations

---

[8] For this publication, the data life cycle is defined as the flow of data from conception through retirement. (Adapted from [ISO/IEC/IEEE 15288]). It includes the set of operations performed upon the data, including but not limited to creation/collection, ingestion, storage, retrieval, alteration, disclosure, dissemination, archiving, and destruction (adapted from [ISO/IEC 29100] definition of "Processing of PII"). It may be applied to all types of data, including electronic data, metadata, sensor data, human knowledge, Personally Identifiable Information (PII), and other data.

Outputs	List of functionalities and capabilities to pass to C.3.
Methods	Document Analysis; Brainstorming; Requirements Definition; Architecture Definition; Data Modeling; Data Flow Diagrams; Survey/Questionnaire.
Related processes outside of criticality analysis	[CSF] – (ID.AM-1, 2, 4) Asset Management [NIST SP 800-39] – (3.1) Framing Risk [NIST SP 800-160] – (3.4.3) System Requirements Definition Process [NIST SP 800-160] – (3.4.4) Architecture Definition Process [NIST SP 800-161] – (2.2.1) Frame

C.3 – Identify Interactions, Intersections, Connections, and Dependencies Within the Critical Workflow Path

Sub-process ID	C.3
Sub-process name	Identify Interactions, Intersections, Connections, and Dependencies Within the Critical Workflow Path
Sub-process description	This sub-process identifies the interactions, intersections, connections, and dependencies between functions and between systems/subsystems. Identify interactions, intersections, connections, and dependencies between functionalities and between system(s)/subsystem(s). Consider assigning initial values to each of the functionalities and capabilities to determine their relationship to a critical workflow path. Identify whether they directly perform tasks to complete an activity on a critical workflow path, perform tasks which support but do not directly complete an activity, or if they are useful to the activity but not vital. Consider under what conditions the functionality or capability would become more or less impactful or valuable. Identify any constraints within the existing infrastructure. Consider identifying the amount of control the organization has over certain dependencies and constraints (e.g., weather). Document this information in a matrix, system diagram, or other representation. Consider grouping or connecting similar or related functions.

Inputs	List of functionalities and capabilities from C.2; Existing Infrastructure and Processes
Outputs	List of interactions, intersections, connections, and dependencies to pass to C.4.
Methods	Document Review; Brainstorming; Questionnaire; Observation; Sensitivity/Uncertainty Analysis
Related processes outside of criticality analysis	[CSF] – (ID.AM-3) Asset Management [NIST SP 800-47] [NIST SP 800-160] – (3.4.3) System Requirements Definition Process [NIST SP 800-160] – (3.4.4) Architecture Definition Process

C.4 – Define Operating States

Sub-process ID	C.4
Sub-process name	Define Operating States
Sub-process description	This sub-process defines scenarios for how the system/subsystem would operate normally and what would constitute abnormal operations of the system/subsystem. Review the functions and capabilities defined in C.2. Describe the condition of the functions and capabilities (i.e., how will it operate). Determine the impact on both the system and the activity the system is intended to support (defined in C.2 and C.3) in each of the following conditions: Non-operational; Impaired (i.e., the function or capability operates at a reduced pace or in an unsafe/insecure/privacy-invasive manner); Normal operation; Increased operations (i.e., the function or capability performs quicker or with more output than normal); and Unintended operations (i.e., the function or capability performs but with additional outputs or actions that are not part of the expected routine). Consider defining what types of scenarios would lead to such situations. Examples of scenarios to consider include reduced performance (e.g., lower

	bandwidth), security breach, privacy problems, physical accident, or any other similar event. Consider the security, safety, and privacy ramifications of these situations. Considerations could include, for example, determining what information would become vulnerable if the function/capability performs slower than normal, what unintended actions could create privacy problems for individuals, could there be physical damages or injury by a function performing too quickly, or how inaccurate or incomplete output caused by software or hardware defects could affect downstream activities. Also consider any contractual, statutory, or other obligations which may be impacted by the operating state.
Inputs	Process Description and/or Diagram; listing of interactions, intersections, connections, and dependencies from C3.
Outputs	Description of operating states to pass to C.5.
Methods	Document Review; Brainstorming; Interviews; Group Decision Making; Scenario/Use Case
Related processes outside of criticality analysis	[NIST SP 800-39] – (3.1) Assessing Risk [NIST SP 800-160] – (3.4.4) Architecture Definition Process [NIST SP 800-161] – (2.2.2) Assess

C.5 – Assign Baseline Criticality Levels to System(s)/Subsystem(s)

Sub-process ID	C.5
Sub-process name	Assign Baseline Criticality Levels to System(s)/Subsystem(s)
Sub-process description	This sub-process determines criticality levels of system(s) and subsystems identified in C.3 against adverse states defined in C.4. Determine the severity of the operating states on the activity that the function/capability is intended to support. Consider: which systems/subsystems perform vital functions and capabilities and would be most impacted by an adverse state, the potential long- or short-term impact(s) of those adverse operating states, the life cycle of the system related to the workflow (e.g. planned end of life or expected end of use for the project), and

	whether the system is continuously in operation or only when certain conditions are met

The user may rank systems and subsystems that are on the critical workflow path. This could be a ranking (e.g., low, moderate, high) or measure (e.g., time lost; cost in time/resources; probability of being able to complete activity). The user could also use ranges and thresholds to define such rankings. |
Inputs	Listing of interactions, intersections, connections, and dependencies from C.3; Listing of adverse states from C.4.
Outputs	Baseline Criticality for each analyzed system/subsystem.
Methods	Document Review; Group Decision Making; Root Cause Analysis; Scenario/Use Case
Related processes outside of criticality analysis	[FIPS 199]

[NIST SP 800-39] – (3.1) Framing Risk

[NIST SP 800-55]

[NIST SP 800-60]

[NIST SP 800-160] – (3.4.1) Business or Mission Analysis Process

[NIST SP 800-160] – (3.4.2) Stakeholder Needs and Requirements Definition Process

[NIST SP 800-161] – (2.2.1) Frame |

3.4   Process D – Conduct Component/Subcomponent-Level Criticality Analysis

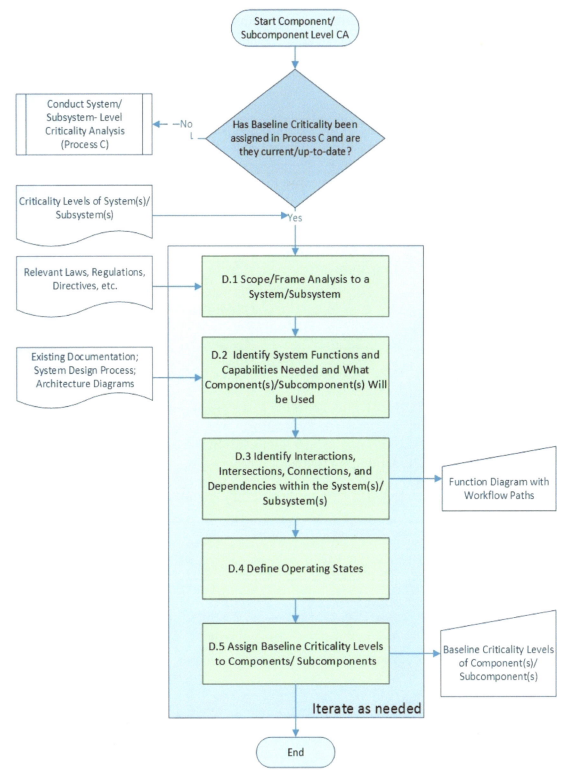

Figure 5 - System/Subsystem-Level Criticality Analysis

Process D, *Conduct Component/Subcomponent-Level Criticality Analysis*, depicted in Figure 5, is ideally performed after Process C, *Conduct System/Subsystem-Level Criticality Analysis*, is complete. It is performed at the component and subcomponent levels, as defined by the user. Often, the components/subcomponents will be COTS products; as a result, this process will likely be performed out of sequence and, at least partially, by a third party. The amount of detail an organization may be able to receive from a third-party supplier regarding the criticality of components/subcomponents may be limited. In these cases, the organization may choose to obtain the information another way (e.g., through extensive testing), obtain contractual assurances that the components will meet the needs of the organization according to the system-level criticality analysis results, or assume that a component is critical and apply appropriate mitigating controls. The process may be repeated at increasingly granular levels to break a complex set of components down into their smallest parts, until the lowest hierarchical level of component is analyzed. As the components could be decomposed into extremely fine detail (e.g., raw materials), it is important to define what level of granularity is necessary for this analysis.

Process D consists of the following:

- Scope/frame the analysis to a specific system or subsystem;
- Identify system functionalities, capabilities, and pathways needed to fulfill functional requirements;
- Match components and subcomponents to the identified system functionalities, capabilities, and pathways;
- Define normal operating conditions and those conditions that system/subsystem will be operating sub-optimally, referred to as adverse operating states; and
- Assign Baseline Criticality to the components and subcomponents identified earlier.

Much of this process is conducted as part of system architecture and design processes.

Process	D
Process name	Conduct Component/Subcomponent-Level Criticality Analysis
Process summary	This process reviews and analyzes a specific system to identify critical components and/or subcomponents.
Inputs	Criticality Levels of System(s)/Subsystem(s); Relevant Laws, Regulations, Directives, etc.; Existing Documentation; System Design Process; Architecture Diagrams
Outputs	Function Diagram with Workflow Pathways; Baseline Criticality Levels of Component(s)/Subcomponent(s)
Roles and Responsibilities	Responsible: Lead System Engineer or a similar role is responsible for the performance of this sub-process. Lead Security Engineer serves as a co-lead

	for sub-processes D.4, Define Operating States, and D.5, Assign Baseline Criticality Levels to Components/Subcomponents. Accountable: Lead System Engineer or a similar role can delegate the execution of this process to another suitable individual, e.g., system analyst. Consulted: Individuals who have detailed knowledge of the activities identified by this process participates in this process to contribute to the identification critical activities. These individuals may include system architects and designers, system engineers, security or privacy engineers, other security or privacy professionals, acquisition/procurement professionals, business leaders, legal experts/general counsel, third-party supplier representatives, and others, as appropriate. Invite representatives of each relevant group to participate in this process. Informed: Individuals responsible for conducting any part of the criticality analysis.
Related processes outside of criticality analysis	[ISO/IEC 12207] [ISO/IEC/IEEE 15288] [NIST SP 800-39] – (3.1) Framing Risk [NIST SP 800-39] – (3.2) Assessing Risk [NIST SP 800-160] – (3.4.4) Architecture Definition Process [NIST SP 800-160] – (3.4.5) Design Definition Process [NIST SP 800-161] – (2.2.1) Frame [NIST SP 800-161] – (2.2.2) Assess

D.1 – Scope/Frame Analysis to a System/Subsystem

Sub-process ID	D.1
Sub-process name	Scope/Frame Analysis to a System/Subsystem
Sub-process description	This sub-process narrows the scope of the analysis to a specific system or subsystem. Ideally, it is performed once Baseline Criticality Levels of systems/subsystems have been determined. If criticality levels have not been determined, strongly consider returning to Process C, *Conduct*

	System/Subsystem-Level Criticality Analysis. In the case of COTS products, the process will likely be performed out of sequence. Using the documentation and criticality levels developed in Process C along with any other relevant laws, regulations, directives, etc., identify which critical system/subsystem are to be further analyzed. For this portion of the criticality analysis, the system/subsystem is an IT/OT product, device, or solution, although the Model will support the analysis of any well-defined system. Separate analyses are conducted for all critical systems identified in Process C, if possible. This is because the components composing systems are often varied even if the systems seem identical. Ensure that the scope has definitive boundaries. Define any assumptions or constraints, which will help limit the analysis. Components and subcomponents are sometimes guided by specific legal and regulatory requirements, such as sourcing requirements (where those can/cannot come from); take those into account. If the analysis is conducted by a third party, such as in the case of COTS, work with the COTS provider(s) to define what information is available which may serve to inform a Baseline Criticality determination, including system documentation, risk analyses performed, operating constraints, and assumptions. If a system does not exist, but is being designed or is under development, bear in mind that the system design may change frequently. It may be best to perform this analysis from a theoretical viewpoint and use the result to inform the design and development process. Then repeat the process as changes to the design occur and when the system development has been completed.
Inputs	Criticality Levels of Systems/Subsystems from Process C; Relevant Laws, Regulations, Directives, and other documents that may contain requirements that describe anything to do with the components that are being used in this system
Outputs	Determination of the system/subsystem to focus analysis
Methods	Document Review; Survey; Interviews
Related processes outside of criticality analysis	[NIST SP 800-39] – (3.1) Framing Risk [NIST SP 800-160] – (3.4.4) Architecture Definition Process [NIST SP 800-160] – (3.4.5) Design Definition Process

	[NIST SP 800-161] – (2.2.1) Frame

D.2 – Identify System Functions and Capabilities Needed and What Components/Subcomponents Will be Used

Sub-process ID	D.2
Sub-process name	Identify System Functions and Capabilities Workflow Needed and What Components/Subcomponents Will be Used
Sub-process description	This sub-process analyzes the system to identify the components and subcomponents required to ensure that the system functions as intended. Review the activities identified in D.1. For existing systems, list the functions and capabilities of the system being analyzed. For systems under development, list functions and capabilities needed. If the system is complex, consider scoping the analysis to only the functions and capabilities determined as critical. Consider configurations, settings, routines, performance parameters, etc. Define the processes or data actions that are activated or that the system uses to perform the identified functions and capabilities. Those processes can be extracted from existing system documentation, such as functional requirements, system diagrams, process flow diagrams, system concept of operations, or any other documentation that describes what the system does. Consider defining what information/data is needed to perform a function: how will that data be processed and how it will be secured. Finally, identify components and subcomponents that are or will be used to support required functionalities and capabilities. If possible, define all of the functions and capabilities of those components and subcomponents; identify which functions or capabilities are not needed or outside the requirements for this particular application. For example, configuration settings or functions that will not be used. Consider the frequency of use of subsystem functions and capabilities and describing end-of-life conditions, such as when the functions/capabilities are expected to no longer be needed, for the system to function.
Inputs	Determination of the system/subsystem from D.1; Existing documentation, system design process, architecture diagrams; existing contractual obligations
Outputs	Listing of capabilities and pathways needed to pass to D.3.

Methods	Document Review; Process Analysis; Systems Analysis; Workflow Analysis; Data Flow Diagrams; Functional Decomposition; Interface Analysis
Related processes outside of criticality analysis	[NIST SP 800-39] – (3.1) Framing Risk [NIST SP 800-160] – (3.4.4) Architecture Definition Process [NIST SP 800-160] – (3.4.5) Design Definition Process [NIST SP 800-161] – (2.2.1) Frame

D.3 – Identify Interactions, Intersections, Connections, and Dependencies Within the System(s)/Subsystem(s)

Sub-process ID	D.3
Sub-process name	Identify Interactions, Intersections, Connections, and Dependencies Within the System(s)/Subsystem(s)
Sub-process description	This sub-process identifies interactions, intersections, connections, and dependencies between components/subcomponents and associated functionalities/capabilities. The way the system uses components and subcomponents to execute a specific function or capability is described as a workflow path. Defined workflow paths may be extremely detailed, including the individual processes used by subcomponents. Note that detailed workflow paths allow for a more accurate and complete criticality analysis, but may not be feasible in many instances. Identify all workflow paths required to execute each system function or, if the system is complex, each critical function. In many cases, a single component, or identical components, will be used to support multiple workflow paths. Document these components matched to workflow paths in a matrix, spreadsheet, database, function diagram, or a similar tool. Identify interactions, intersections, connections, and dependencies between the components. Identify any constraints within the existing infrastructure. Consider identifying the amount of control the organization has over certain dependencies and constraints (e.g., weather). Consider defining triggers or conditions which activate/deactivate the use of a component or which impact how a component is used.

Inputs	Listing of capabilities and pathways from D.2.
	Existing documentation, system design, lists of components, bill of materials, or other documentation that somehow describes components and subcomponents.
Outputs	Listing of components and subcomponents matched to workflow paths to pass to D.4 and D.5; Function Diagram with Workflow Paths
Methods	Document Review; Systems Analysis; Brainstorming; Sensitivity/Uncertainty Analysis
Related processes outside of criticality analysis	[NIST SP 800-39] – (3.1) Framing Risk [NIST SP 800-160] – (3.4.4) Architecture Definition Process [NIST SP 800-160] – (3.4.5) Design Definition Process [NIST SP 800-161] – (2.2.1) Frame

D.4 – Define Operating States

Sub-process ID	D.4
Sub-process name	Define Operating States
Sub-process description	This sub-process defines normal operational states, as well as the states in which the system will be operating abnormally. Review the outputs of D.3. Describe operation of the components and/or workflow paths. Then determine the impact of the various operating states of the component on the workflow path(s), and consequently on the system function/capability that path supports. Consider each of the following operating states: Non-operational; Impaired (i.e., the component/subcomponent operates at a reduced capability or in an unsafe/insecure/privacy-invasive manner); Normal operation; Increased operations (i.e., the function or capability performs quicker or with more output than normal); and Unintended operations (i.e., the function or capability performs but with additional outputs or actions that are not part of the expected routine).

	Consider defining what types of scenarios would lead to such situations. Examples of scenarios to consider include reduced performance (e.g., lower bandwidth), security breach, physical accident, insertion of counterfeit part, or any other similar event. Using the Function Diagram with Workflow Paths, identify specific points within the workflow paths where the system will be particularly stressed as a result of any of these operating states. This would include any points that would exacerbate the situation. Define the severity of the impact of the operating states. This may be a ranking (e.g., low, moderate, high) or measure (e.g., processing speed; downtime; percentage of remaining functionality). Consider the security, safety, and privacy ramifications of these situations; for example, what information is made vulnerable if the components/subcomponents fail? Could the data processing create privacy problems for individuals? Also consider any contractual, statutory, or other obligations which may be impacted by the operating state. Consider the lifetime of the component/subcomponent and the duration of an adverse operating state. Often, the impact of an adverse operating state is more severe over a longer time frame.
Inputs	Listing of components and subcomponents matched to workflow paths from D.3; Function Diagram with Workflow Paths
Outputs	Description of operating states to pass to D.5.
Methods	Document Review; Systems Analysis; Workflow Analysis; Brainstorming; Group Decision Making; Scenario/Use Case
Related processes outside of criticality analysis	[NIST SP 800-39] – (3.2) Assessing Risk [NIST SP 800-160] – (3.4.5) Design Definition Process [NIST SP 800-161] – (2.2.2) Assess

D.5 – Assign Baseline Criticality Levels to Components/Subcomponents

Sub-process ID	D.5
Sub-process name	Assign Baseline Criticality Levels to Components/Subcomponents

Sub-process description	This sub-process assigns criticality levels to components and subcomponents identified in D.3 based on the impact of the operating states defined in D.4. Rank the components and subcomponents in a way that gives the highest ranking to components and subcomponents that are on the critical workflow path, perform vital functions and capabilities, and would be most impacted by adverse operating states. The user can create a ranking schema that would, for example, rank those activities and workflow paths that are impacted by the highest number of scenarios as "High Criticality" and those that are impacted by the lowest number of scenarios as "Low Criticality." The user could also use ranges and thresholds to define such rankings.
Inputs	Listing of components and subcomponents matched to workflow paths from D.3; Function Diagram with Workflow Paths; Description of operating states from D.4.
Outputs	Baseline Criticality Levels of Component(s)/Subcomponent(s)
Methods	Document Review; Systems Analysis; Process Flow Analysis; Group Decision Making; Root Cause Analysis; Scenario/Use Case
Related processes outside of criticality analysis	[FIPS 199] [NIST SP 800-39] – (3.1) Framing Risk [NIST SP 800-161] – (2.2.1) Frame

3.5 Process E – Conduct Detailed Review of Criticality for Processes B, C, and D

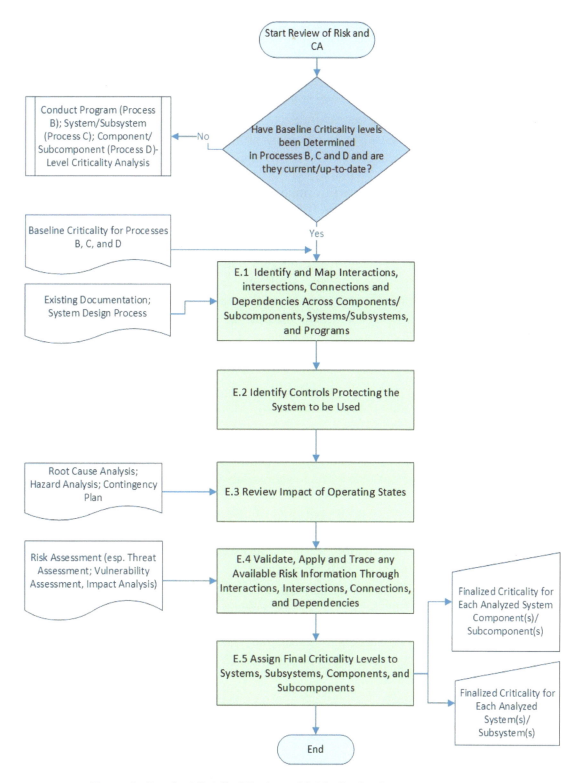

Figure 6 - Conduct Detailed Review of Criticality for Processes B, C, and D

Process E, *Conduct Detailed Review of Criticality for Processes B, C, and D*, depicted in Figure 6, provides a bottom-up review of impacts and ensures cross-process interaction and collaboration. Process E consists of the following:

- Identify and map interactions, intersections, connections, and dependencies across Program; System/Subsystem; or Component/Subcomponent;
- Identify controls protecting the system to be used;
- Review impact of operating states; and
- Validate, apply, and trace any available risk information through interactions, intersections, connections, and dependencies.

Process E is a bottom-up process where information is iteratively validated across the entire Model. Process E is performed after sub-processes B.5, C.5, and D.5. The output of these sub-processes, Baseline Criticality, is used as an input to Process E.

The information on Baseline Criticality for components/subcomponents is used to validate criticality for systems/subsystems. Please note that program-level baseline criticality does not need to be revised here and is an input only. This process iterates until the three criticalities are consistent and harmonized. When the validation is complete, the user can finalize criticality levels for systems/subsystems and components/subcomponents.

Process	E
Process name	Conduct Detailed Review of Criticality for Processes B, C, and D
Process summary	This is a bottom-up sub-process conducted after Baseline Criticality levels have been defined under Processes B, C and D. It is used to create final criticality levels for Systems/Subsystems and Components/Subcomponents. This process involves identifying interactions, intersections, connections, and dependencies across Processes B, C, and D. It considers any available risk information, including any existing mitigation strategies, to create a more precise criticality score.
Inputs	Baseline Criticality for B, C, and D; Existing Documentation; System Design Process; Security Requirements; Functional Requirements; Root Cause Analysis; Hazard Analysis; Risk Assessment (esp. Threat Assessment; Vulnerability Assessment, Impact Analysis, Privacy Risk Assessment)
Outputs	Criticality Levels of Programs, Systems/Subsystems, and Component(s)/ Subcomponent(s)
Roles and Responsibilities	Responsible: Lead System Architect or a similar role is responsible for the performance of this sub-process. Lead Security Engineer serves as a co-lead for this process.

	Accountable: Lead System Engineer should work in partnership with Lead Security or Privacy Engineer and Program Manager to ensure appropriate communication and collaboration across Processes B, C, and D. Consulted: Individuals who have detailed knowledge of the activities identified by this process should participate in this process to contribute to the identification of critical activities. These individuals may include system architects and designers, system engineers, security or privacy engineers, other security or privacy professionals, acquisition/procurement professionals, business leaders, and others, as appropriate. Identify representatives of each relevant group to participate in this process. Informed: Individuals responsible for conducting any part of the criticality analysis.
Related processes outside of criticality analysis	[FIPS 199] [NIST SP 800-39] – (3.2) Assessing Risk [NIST SP 800-160] – (3.4.4) Architecture Definition Process [NIST SP 800-160] – (3.4.5) Design Definition Process [NIST SP 800-161] – (2.2.2) Assess (Risk Assessment, Threat Assessment; Vulnerability Assessment, Impact Analysis)

E.1 – Identify and Map Interactions, Intersections, Connections, and Dependencies Across Components/ Subcomponents, Systems/Subsystems, and Programs

Sub-process ID	E.1
Sub-process name	Identify and Map Interactions, Intersections, Connections, and Dependencies Across Components/ Subcomponents, Systems/Subsystems, and Programs
Sub-process description	This sub-process uses the process diagrams, design documents, or other artifacts created in processes B, C, and D, to trace subcomponents through to program goals and objectives. One system component or type of system component may be used in multiple subsystems. Identify these by reviewing the system design documentation that was created in Process D for each system or subsystem that was identified in Process C.

	Similarly, one system may support multiple programs. Identify these by reviewing the systems identified in Process C for each workflow described in Process B. Identify identical or similar types of components used for critical functions of multiple systems. Also, identify components or subsystems that originate from a single supplier. Look for any other connection or dependency that may impact the success of the objective or goals if stretched by maintenance, supply chain, security, or other concerns.
Inputs	Baseline Criticality Levels of Program, System(s)/Subsystem(s), and Component(s)/ Subcomponent(s); Existing Documentation and System Design Process
Outputs	Identification and maps of interactions, intersections, connections, and dependencies across Program, System/Subsystem, and Component/Subcomponent to pass to E.2.
Methods	Document Review; Mission Thread Analysis; Impact Analysis; Hazard Analysis
Related processes outside of criticality analysis	[CSF] – (ID.AM-3) Asset Management [FIPS 199] [NIST SP 800-39] – (3.2) Assess Risk [NIST SP 800-47] [NIST SP 800-160] – (3.4.4) Architecture Definition Process [NIST SP 800-160] – (3.4.5) Design Definition Process [NIST SP 800-161] – (2.2.2) Assess (Risk Assessment, Threat Assessment; Vulnerability Assessment, Impact Analysis)

E.2 – Identify Controls Protecting the System to Be Used

Sub-process ID	E.2
Sub-process name	Identify controls protecting the system to be used.
Sub-process description	This sub-process is used to identify components, system functions, processes, or other measures that are used to ensure that the system operates within acceptable parameters.

	Beginning at the subcomponent level, identify all controls that ensure that the program, systems, and components operate within acceptable parameters. Identify system components that monitor or protect critical subcomponents. Then review critical components and identify any system functions that provide those same assurances. Next, identify external systems, programmatic activities, processes, procedures, and practices that serve to monitor or protect the system. Identify any programmatic activities that serve to monitor or protect the program itself. Using the interactions, intersections, connections, and dependencies identified in E.1, *Identify and Map Interactions, Intersections, Connections, and Dependencies across Program, System/Subsystem, and Component/Subcomponent*, identify controls that monitor and protect those interactions, intersections, connections, and dependencies.
Inputs	Identification and maps of interactions, intersections, connections, and dependencies across Program, System/Subsystem, and Component/Subcomponent from E.1; Security Requirements; Functional Requirements
Outputs	Listing of controls protecting the system to be used to pass to E.3.
Methods	Document Review; Security and Privacy Control Selection and Allocation (Risk Management)
Related processes outside of criticality analysis	[CSF] – (ID.GV) Governance; (ID.RA-6) Risk Assessment; (ID.RM) Risk Management Strategy [FIPS 199] [ISO/IEC 22301] [ISO/IEC 27001] [NIST SP 800-34] [NIST SP 800-39] – (3.2) Assess Risk [NIST SP 800-160] – (3.4.4) Architecture Definition Process [NIST SP 800-160] – (3.4.5) Design Definition Process [NIST SP 800-161] – (2.2.2) Assess (Risk Assessment, Threat Assessment; Vulnerability Assessment, Impact Analysis)

E.3 – Review Impact of Operating States

Sub-process ID	E.3
Sub-process name	Review Impact of Operating States
Sub-process description	Beginning at the subcomponent level, trace the impact of each adverse operating state at the system level (defined in C.4) would have on the operations of the activity or workflow path it is meant to support (defined in B), and what each adverse operating state at the activity level would have on the success of the program (defined in B.4).
	Using the controls identified in E.2, review the likelihood of the adverse operating states and associated impact(s) occurring. For example, if there are no controls monitoring and protecting a vital component, this may need to be reflected in the criticality level of the component.
	Consider frequency of use of components/systems and describing end-of-life conditions such as when the components/systems are expected to no longer be needed or critical to the project.
Inputs	Listing of controls protecting the system to be used from E.2; Descriptions of operating states from B.4, C.4, and D.4; Results of Root Cause Analysis; Results of Hazard Analysis; Contingency Plans
Outputs	Refined list of operating states to pass to E.4.
Methods	Document Analysis; Scenario/Use Case; Hazard Analysis
Related processes outside of criticality analysis	[CSF] – (ID.RA-4) Risk Assessment
	[FIPS 199]
	[NISTIR 8062]
	[NIST SP 800-39] – (3.2) Assess Risk
	[NIST SP 800-160] – (3.4.4) Architecture Definition Process
	[NIST SP 800-160] – (3.4.5) Design Definition Process
	[NIST SP 800-161] – (2.2.2) Assess (Risk Assessment, Threat Assessment; Vulnerability Assessment, Impact Analysis)

E.4 – Validate, Apply and Trace any Available Risk Information Through Interactions, Intersections, Connections, and Dependencies

Sub-process ID	E.4
Sub-process name	Validate, Apply and Trace any Available Risk Information Through Interactions, Intersections, Connections, and Dependencies
Sub-process description	If available, apply any threat, vulnerability, problematic data action, or other risk information to the interactions, intersections, connections, and dependencies mapping. Include supply chain, cybersecurity, privacy, and any other applicable risks. Apply any updated criticality information from processes B, C, and D, and increase or decrease the criticality level of the system or component as appropriate.
Inputs	Refined list of adverse operating states from E.3; Risk Assessment (esp. Threat Assessment; Vulnerability Assessment, Impact Analysis).
Outputs	Detailed review results to pass to E.5, *Assign Final Criticality Levels to Systems, Subsystems, Components, and Subcomponents.*
Methods	Document Review; Risk Analysis; Brainstorming
Related processes outside of criticality analysis	[CSF] – (ID.RA) Risk Assessment [FIPS 199] [NIST SP 800-39] – (3.2) Assess Risk [NIST SP 800-160] – (3.4.4) Architecture Definition Process [NIST SP 800-160] – (3.4.5) Design Definition Process [NIST SP 800-161] – (2.2.2) Assess (Risk Assessment, Threat Assessment; Vulnerability Assessment, Impact Analysis)

E.5 – Assign Final Criticality Levels to Systems, Subsystems, Components, and Subcomponents

Sub-process ID	E.5
Sub-process name	Assign Final Criticality Levels to Systems, Subsystems, Components, and Subcomponents

Sub-process description	This sub-process finalizes Baseline Criticality levels determined in processes C and D. The critical nature of components and systems may be influenced by the interactions, intersections, connections, and dependencies, connections, controls, frequency of use, and impacts identified in Process E. Review the Baseline Criticality levels defined in C.5 and D.5. Considering the outputs of Process E, refine the rankings. Consider ranking: Components and subcomponents by their importance in keeping the system from entering adverse operating states or keeping the system operational while in adverse operating states; and Systems and subsystems by their importance in keeping the program from entering adverse operating states or keeping the program running while in adverse operating states. Avoid reducing the criticality scores of systems and components without carefully considering legal, regulatory, safety, security, privacy, business, and other constraints and managerial decisions. A concatenated score may be used (e.g. using a scale 1 to 5, a combined score of 1.3.2 may show that a component has a "2" rating in a "3" system in a "1" project). Note that when components support multiple systems, it can be useful to track the criticality of that component to each project in addition to its finalized criticality level. A scoring system may be defined that uses the information from Process E to refine but not alter the Baseline Criticality levels. For example, Baseline Criticality levels could be given a digit identifier from 1 to 5 while results of the review conducted in Process E could add a digit 0 to 9 to that identifier, to make the final identifier a two-digit ranking from 10 to 59. Whatever method is used to score the criticality levels, ensure that the method is sufficiently detailed so that a reasonably small number of components are given a high criticality score. The process described in this publication usually will not result in a large number of components being given a high criticality score. If this occurs, it may be assumed that many of these components are either outside the scope or control of the program or do not have highest criticality. In general, a component is not given a higher criticality level than the highest criticality of the systems it supports. Neither would a system have a higher criticality level than the highest criticality of the processes/workflow paths it supports. Determine the duration for the final criticality level to be valid. Consider the life cycle of the components, systems, and projects under evaluation.

	As part of the risk management process related to the system/components, define means to monitor changes to the system and component criticality levels over the life cycle of the project and over the life cycle of those components and systems.
Inputs	Detailed Review Results from Sub-Process E, *Conduct Detailed Review of Risk and Criticality Analysis.*
Outputs	Finalized criticality for each analyzed component/subcomponent, system/subsystem, etc.
Methods	Document Review; Brainstorming; Group Decision Making
Related processes outside of criticality analysis	[CSF] – (ID.AM-5) Asset Management [FIPS 199] [NIST SP 800-39] – (3.2) Assess Risk [NIST SP 800-160] – (3.4.1) Business or Mission Analysis Process [NIST SP 800-160] – (3.4.2) Stakeholder Needs and Requirements Definition Process [NIST SP 800-160] – (3.4.4) Architecture Definition Process [NIST SP 800-160] – (3.4.5) Design Definition Process [NIST SP 800-161] – (2.2.2) Assess

Appendix A—Acronyms

Selected acronyms and abbreviations used in this paper are defined below.

BABOK	Business Analysis Body of Knowledge
CA	Criticality Analysis
COTS	Commercial Off-the-Shelf
DoD	Department of Defense
FIPS	Federal Information Processing Standard
FMECA	Failure Mode Effects and Criticality Analysis
GRAI-GIM	Graphs with Results and Actions Inter-related Integrated Methodology
HVA	High Value Asset
INCOSE	International Council on Systems Engineering
ISO	International Organization for Standardization
ISO/IEC	International Organization for Standardization/International Electrotechnical Commission
ISO/IEC/IEEE	International Organization for Standardization/International Electrotechnical Commission/ Institute of Electrical and Electronics Engineers
IT	Information Technology
IT SCRM	Information Technology Supply Chain Risk Management
ITL	Information Technology Laboratory
IT/OT	Information Technology/Operational Technology
NIST	National Institute of Standards and Technology
NIST SP	National Institute of Standards and Technology Special Publication
NISTIR	National Institute of Standards and Technology Interagency Report
OT	Operational Technology
PMBOK	Project Management Body of Knowledge

SP	Special Publication
SCRM	Supply Chain Risk Management
SOS	System of Systems
US	United States

Appendix B—References

Sources for the Model

[1]   International Institute of Business Analysis, *A Guide to the Business Analysis Body of Knowledge (BABOK Guide) v. 3,* April 15, 2015.

[2]   Warwick Manufacturing Group, *Product Excellence Using Six Sigma, Section 12: Failure Modes, Effects & Criticality Analysis, University of Warwick, Coventry, CV4 7AL, UK,* 32pp, http://www2.warwick.ac.uk/fac/sci/wmg/ftmsc/modules/modulelist/peuss/slides/section_12a_fmeca_Notes.pdf [accessed 4/3/2018].

[3]   H. Salim, *Cyber Safety: A Systems Thinking and Systems Theory Approach to Managing Cyber Security Risks,* Working Paper CISL# 2014-07, Massachusetts Institute of Technology, Cambridge, MA, September 2014, 157 pp, http://web.mit.edu/smadnick/www/wp/2014-07.pdf [accessed 4/3/2018].

[4]   H. Salim and S. Madnick, *Cyber Safety: A Systems Theory Approach to Managing Cyber Security Risks – Applied to TJX Cyber Attack,* Working Paper CISL# 2016-09, Massachusetts Institute of Technology, Cambridge, MA, August 2016, 17pp, http://web.mit.edu/smadnick/www/wp/2016-09.pdf [accessed 4/3/2018].

[5]   N. Leveson, *An STPA Primer, Version 1*, August 2013, 80pp, http://sunnyday.mit.edu/STPA-Primer-v0.pdf [accessed 4/3/2018].

[6]   N. Leveson, *Engineering a Safer and More Secure World*, MIT Press, June 2011, 72pp http://psas.scripts.mit.edu/home/wp-content/uploads/2016/04/STAMP-Intro-2016.pdf [accessed 4/3/2018].

[7]   D. Reddy, "Criticality Analysis & Supply Chain: Providing Representational Assurance," paper presented at the RSA Conference, Moscone Center, San Francisco, February 24-28, 2014, https://www.rsaconference.com/writable/presentations/file_upload/str-w04a-criticality-analysis-supply-chain_v2.pdf [accessed 4/3/2018].

[8]   D. Reddy, "Criticality analysis and the supply chain: Leveraging representational assurance," *Technovation* 34(7), July 2014, pp. 362-379. https://doi.org/10.1016/j.technovation.2014.01.009.

[9]   National Electric Sector Cybersecurity Organization Resource (NESCOR), *Electric Sector Failure Scenarios and Impact Analyses – Version 3.0,* December 2015, http://smartgrid.epri.com/doc/NESCOR%20Failure%20Scenarios%20v3%2012-11-15.pdf [accessed 4/3/2018].

[10]   INCOSE, *INCOSE Systems Engineering Handbook: A Guide for System Life Cycle Processes and Activities,* 4th Edition, [New York: Wiley, 2015], Chapters 4, 6, 10.

[11]   Department of Defense, *Defense Acquisition Guidebook: Chapter 13 – Program Protection Plan,* March 2012, 70pp.

[12]   M. Reed, "System Security Engineering and Comprehensive Program Protection," presented at the 16th Annual NDIA Systems Engineering Conference, Arlington, VA, October 30, 2013 (Revised 4/17/2104), http://www.acq.osd.mil/se/briefs/2013_10_30_NDIA-SEC-Reed-ProgramProtection-Approved.pdf [accessed 4/3/2018].

[13]   M. Reed, "Comprehensive Program Protection Planning for the Materiel Solution Analysis (MSA) Phase," presented at the 15th Annual NDIA Systems Engineering Conference, San Diego, CA, October 24, 2012, http://www.acq.osd.mil/se/briefs/14761-2012_10_24-NDIA-SEC-Reed-SSE-PP-MSA-Phase.pdf [accessed 4/3/2018].

[14]   J.C. Franchitti, *Session 1 – Sub-Topic 1Requirements Definition & Management Processes and Tools,* Software Engineering, G22.2440-001, New York University, 21pp, http://www.nyu.edu/classes/jcf/g22.2440-001_sp09/slides/session2/g22_2440_001_c22.pdf [accessed 4/3/2018].

[15]   A Guide to Fault Detection and Diagnosis, Greg Stanley and Associates [Website] http://gregstanleyandassociates.com/whitepapers/FaultDiagnosis/faultdiagnosis.htm [accessed 4/3/2018].

[16]   SAE International, *ARP4761, Guidelines and Methods for Conducting the Safety Assessment Process on Civil Airborne Systems and Equipment,* 331pp, December 1, 1996, http://standards.sae.org/arp4761/ [accessed 4/3/2018].

[17]   Creating A Value Stream Map, Lean Manufacturing Tools [Website], http://leanmanufacturingtools.org/551/creating-a-value-stream-map/ [accessed 4/3/2018].

[18]   Value-Stream Mapping for Manufacturing, Lean Enterprise Institute [Website], https://www.lean.org/Workshops/WorkshopDescription.cfm?WorkshopId=7 [accessed 4/3/2018].

[19]   Factor Analysis of Information Risk, FAIR Institute [Website], http://www.fairinstitute.org [accessed 4/3/2018].

[20]   Merriam-Webster [Website], https://www.merriam-webster.com/dictionary/ [accessed 4/3/2018].

[21]   R.K. McAllister and J. L. Coyle. "Interdependency analysis," Proceedings of the 22nd National Information Systems Security Conference, Arlington, Virginia, October 18-21, 1999, pp. 403-414. https://csrc.nist.gov/csrc/media/publications/conference-

paper/1999/10/21/proceedings-of-the-22nd-nissc-1999/documents/papers/p31.pdf,
[accessed 4/3/2018].

[22]   M. Gagliardi, W. Wood and T. Morrow, *Introduction to the Mission Thread
         Workshop*, Carnegie Mellon University, Software Engineering Institute, CMU/SEI-
         2013-TR-003 Software Engineering Institute, October 2013, 44 pp,
         http://repository.cmu.edu/cgi/viewcontent.cgi?article=1762&context=sei [accessed
         4/3/2018].

[23]   Project Management Institute, *Project Management Body of Knowledge (PMBOK
         Guide) 5th edition,* 2014.

[24]   What is a Process Flowchart?, American Society for Quality (ASQ) [Website],
         http://asq.org/learn-about-quality/process-analysis-tools/overview/flowchart.html
         [accessed 4/3/2018].

[25]   Six Sigma Daily [Website], http://www.sixsigmadaily.com/ [accessed 4/3/2018].

[26]   U.S. Department of Transportation Pipeline and Hazardous Materials Safety
         Administration [Website], https://www.phmsa.dot.gov/ [accessed 4/3/2018].

[27]   The Open Group, *The Open Group Architecture Framework TOGAF*, *Version 9,*
         2009.

[28]   U.S. Department of Health and Human Services, *Enterprise Performance Life Cycle
         Framework Practices Guide: Requirements Definition*, [Website]
         https://www.hhs.gov/sites/default/files/ocio/eplc-lifecycle-framework.pdf [accessed
         4/3/2018].

[29]   Healthcare Information and Management Systems Society (HIMSS) [Website],
         http://www.himss.org/ [accessed 4/3/2018].

[30]   K. Eliaz, D. Ray and R. Razin, "Group decision-making in the shadow of
         disagreement," *Journal of Economic Theory* 132(1), January 2007, pp. 236-273.
         https://doi.org/10.1016/j.jet.2005.07.008.

[31]   D. Chen and G. Doumeingts, "The GRAI-GIM reference model, architecture and
         methodology," *Architectures for Enterprise Integration*. IFIP Advances in
         Information and Communication Technology, Springer: Boston, MA, 1996, pp.
         102-126, https://doi.org/10.1007/978-0-387-34941-1_7.

[32]   C. Cacuci, "Sensitivity and Uncertainty Analysis Theory," Volume 1, Chapman &
         Hall/CRC (2003), http://inis.jinr.ru/sl/tot_ra/0/0/3/Cacuci-Sensitiv.pdf [accessed
         4/3/2018].

Related Standards and NIST Publications

[CNSSI 4009]   Committee on National Security Systems Instruction (CNSSI) No. 4009, *Committee on National Security Systems (CNSS) Glossary*, April 2015

[CSF]   National Institute of Standards and Technology, *Framework for Improving Critical Infrastructure Cybersecurity. Version 1.0*, February 12, 2014, 41pp, https://doi.org/10.6028/NIST.CSWP.02122014 .

[FIPS 199]   Federal Information Processing Standards Publication (FIPS PUB) 199, *Standards for Security Categorization of Federal Information and Information Systems*, National Institute of Standards and Technology, Gaithersburg, Maryland, February 2004, 13pp. https://doi.org/10.6028/NIST.FIPS.199.

[ISO 21500]   International Organization for Standardization, *Guidance on Project Management*, ISO 21500:2012, 2012, https://www.iso.org/standard/50003.html.

[ISO/IEC 12207]   International Organization for Standardization/International Electrotechnical Commission/ Institute of Electrical and Electronics Engineers, *Systems and software engineering -- Software life cycle processes*, ISO/IEC 12207:2017, 2017. https://www.iso.org/standard/63712.html.

[ISO/IEC 20243]   International Organization for Standardization/International Electrotechnical Commission, *Information technology – Open Trusted Technology ProviderTM Standard (O-TTPS) -- Mitigating maliciously tainted and counterfeit products*, ISO/IEC 20243:2015, 2015, https://www.iso.org/standard/67394.html.

[ISO/IEC 22301]   International Organization for Standardization, *Societal security -- Business continuity management systems --- Requirements*, ISO 22301:2012, 2012, https://www.iso.org/standard/50038.html.

[ISO/IEC 27001]   International Organization for Standardization/International Electrotechnical Commission, *Information technology – Security techniques – Information security management system – Requirements*, ISO/IEC 27001:2013, 2013, https://www.iso.org/standard/54534.html.

[ISO/IEC 27002]   International Organization for Standardization/International Electrotechnical Commission, *Information technology – Security techniques – Code of practice for information security controls*, ISO/IEC 27002:2013, 2013, https://www.iso.org/standard/54533.html.

[ISO/IEC 27036]   International Organization for Standardization/International Electrotechnical Commission, *Information technology – Security techniques – Information security for supplier relationships – Part 1: Overview and concepts*, ISO/IEC 27036-1:2014, 2014, https://www.iso.org/standard/59648.html.

[ISO/IEC 29100]	International Organization for Standardization/International Electrotechnical Commission, *Information technology – Security techniques – Privacy Framework*, ISO/IEC 29100:2011, 2011, https://www.iso.org/standard/45123.html.
[ISO/IEC/ IEEE 15288]	International Organization for Standardization/International Electrotechnical Commission/ Institute of Electrical and Electronics Engineers, *Information technology – System and software life cycle processes*, ISO/IEC/IEEE 15288:2015, 2015, https://www.iso.org/standard/63711.html.
[NIST SP 800-160]	NIST Special Publication (SP) 800-160 Volume 1, *Systems Security Engineering Considerations for a Multidisciplinary Approach in the Engineering of Trustworthy Secure Systems,* National Institute of Standards and Technology, Gaithersburg, Maryland, November 2017 (updated 3/21/2018), 260pp, https://doi.org/10.6028/NIST.SP.800-160v1.
[NIST SP 800-161]	NIST Special Publication (SP) 800-161, *Supply Chain Risk Management Practices for Federal Information Systems and Organizations*, National Institute of Standards and Technology, Gaithersburg, Maryland, April 2015, 282pp, https://doi.org/10.6028/NIST.SP.800-161.
[NIST SP 800-181]	NIST Special Publication (SP) 800-181, *National Initiative for Cybersecurity Education (NICE) Cybersecurity Workforce Framework*, National Institute of Standards and Technology, Gaithersburg, Maryland, August 2017, 135pp, https://doi.org/10.6028/NIST.SP.800-181.
[NIST SP 800-30]	NIST Special Publication (SP) 800-30 Revision 1, *Guide for Conducting Risk Assessments*, National Institute of Standards and Technology, Gaithersburg, Maryland, September 2012, 95pp, https://doi.org/10.6028/NIST.SP.800-30r1.
[NIST SP 800-34]	NIST Special Publication (SP) 800-34 Revision 1, *Contingency Planning Guide for Federal Information Systems,* National Institute of Standards and Technology, Gaithersburg, Maryland, November 2010, 149pp, https://doi.org/10.6028/NIST.SP.800-34r1.
[NIST SP 800-37]	NIST Special Publication (SP) 800-37 Revision 1, *Guide for Applying the Risk Management Framework to Federal Information Systems: A Security Life Cycle Approach,* National Institute of Standards and Technology, Gaithersburg, Maryland, June 2014, 102pp, https://doi.org/10.6028/NIST.SP.800-37r1.
[NIST SP 800-39]	NIST Special Publication (SP) 800-39, *Managing Information Security Risk: Organization, Mission, and Information System View,* National Institute of Standards and Technology, Gaithersburg, Maryland, March 2011, 88pp, https://doi.org/10.6028/NIST.SP.800-39.
[NIST SP 800-47]	NIST Special Publication (SP) 800-47, *Security Guide for Interconnecting Information Technology Systems,* National Institute of Standards and Technology,

Gaithersburg, Maryland, September 2002, 58pp,
https://doi.org/10.6028/NIST.SP.800-47.

[NIST SP 800-53]   NIST Special Publication (SP) 800-53 Revision 4, *Security and Privacy Controls for Federal Information Systems and Organizations,* National Institute of Standards and Technology, Gaithersburg, Maryland, April 2013 (updated 1/15/2014), 462pp, https://doi.org/10.6028/NIST.SP.800-53r4.

[NIST SP 800-53A]   NIST Special Publication (SP) 800-53A Revision 4, *Assessing Security and Privacy Controls in Federal Information Systems and Organizations: Building Effective Assessment Plans,* National Institute of Standards and Technology, Gaithersburg, Maryland, December 2014 (updated 12/18/2014), 487pp, https://doi.org/10.6028/NIST.SP.800-53Ar4.

[NIST SP 800-55]   NIST Special Publication (SP) 800-55 Revision 1, *Performance Measurement Guide for Information Security,* National Institute of Standards and Technology, Gaithersburg, Maryland, July 2008, 80pp, https://doi.org/10.6028/NIST.SP.800-55r1.

[NIST SP 800-60]   NIST Special Publication (SP) 800-60 Volume 1, Revision 1, *Guide for Mapping Types of Information and Information Systems to Security Categories*, National Institute of Standards and Technology, Gaithersburg, Maryland, August 2008, 53pp, http://doi.org/10.6028/NIST.SP.800-60v1r1.

[NISTIR 8062]   NISTIR 8062, *An Introduction to Privacy Engineering and Risk Management in Federal Systems*, National Institute of Standards and Technology, Gaithersburg, Maryland, January 2017, 49pp, https://doi.org/10.6028/NIST.IR.8062.

Appendix C—Methods

This appendix does not give detailed information on any given method, but provides a short description and reference where more information can be found on how to perform the method.

Activity Network Diagram – "an activity network diagram, also known as arrow diagram, pert chart, and critical path method, is used to show activities that are in parallel and/or in series. It will show the most likely times, the most pessimistic times, and the most likely times for the completion of projects." [25]

Architecture Definition – "provides a formal model of the Baseline Architecture, Target Architecture, and the gaps between the two states." [27]

Brainstorming or Brainstorming of Activities – "a team activity that seeks to produce a broad or diverse set of options through the rapid and uncritical generation of ideas." [1]

Context Diagram – "an analysis model that illustrates product scope by showing the system in its environment with the external entities (people and systems) that give to and receive from the system." [1]

Security Control Selection and Allocation – A process for identifying what security measures are or will be taken. [NIST SP 800-37]

Critical Function Identification – method to identify critical functions in a system/subsystem [11]

Data Flow Diagrams – "an analysis model that illustrates processes that occur, along with the flows of data to and from those processes." [1]

Data Modeling – describes the concepts and relationships relevant to the solution or business domain. [1]

Decision Analysis – "an approach to decision-making that examines and models the possible consequences of different decisions. Decision analysis assists in making an optimal decision under conditions of uncertainty." [1]

Document Analysis – "a means to elicit requirements of an existing system by studying available documentation and identifying relevant information." [1]

Document Review – data collection method for the review of documentation received throughout the criticality analysis process(es)/sub-process(es). This may involve the review of an intranet site, document management system, or use of a librarian or other document management specialist. [1]

Functional Decomposition – to decompose processes, functional areas, or deliverables into their component parts and allow each part to be analyzed independently. [1]

Gantt Chart – a visual representation of a project schedule. A Gantt chart is a type of bar chart in which a series of horizontal lines shows the amount of work done or production completed in certain periods of time in relation to the amount planned for those periods. [23]

GRAI-GIM – methodology "developed to help the designer to model a Production Management System." [31]

Group Decision Making (also known as collaborative decision-making) – "process by which a collective of individuals attempt to reach a required level of consensus on a given issue." [30]

Hazard Analysis – "the identification of material properties, system elements, or events that lead to harm or loss. The term *hazard analysis* may also include evaluation of consequences from an event or incident." [26]

Interdependency Analysis – "a technique for evaluating security service strengths of combinations of security mechanisms employed to protect information. Such a technique can provide a valuable tool for assessing the security architectures and implementations of information systems." [21]

Interface Analysis – elicitation technique used "to identify interfaces between solutions and/or solution components and define requirements that describe how they will interact." [1]

Interviews – "a systematic approach designed to elicit information from a person or group of people in an informal or formal setting by talking to an interviewee, asking relevant questions and documenting the responses." [1]

Mission Thread Analysis – analysis of mission threads. [11]

"Mission Thread – A sequence of end-to-end activities and events that take place to accomplish the execution an SoS capability. The context of a mission thread is defined by a vignette. A mission thread is given as a series of steps. There are three main types of mission thread: operational, development, and sustainment. Chairman of the Joint Chiefs of Staff 6212.01F defines a Joint Mission Thread (JMT) as an operational and technical description of the end-to-end set of activities and systems that accomplish the execution of a joint mission (CJCSI 2012)." [22]

Observation – "a means to elicit requirements by conducting an assessment of the stakeholder's work environment." [1]

Procedure Development – system of creating defined steps and tasks to complete a task performed.

Process Analysis – See workflow analysis.

Process Flow Analysis – analysis of the process flow or workflow diagram.

Process Flow Diagram – Also called process flowchart. "A flowchart is a picture of the separate steps of a process in sequential order. Elements that may be included are: sequence of actions, materials or services entering or leaving the process (inputs and outputs), decisions that must be made, people who become involved, time involved at each step, and/or process measurements. [24]

Project Plan – "a formal, approved document used to guide both project execution and project control. The primary uses of the project plan are to document planning assumptions and decisions, to facilitate communication among stakeholders, and to document approved scope, cost, and schedule baselines. A project plan may be summary or detailed." [23]

Project Planning – "development and maintenance of the project plan." [23]

Process Visualization – See Visualization.

Questionnaire – See Survey.

Requirements Definition – "often the main practice that serves as a bridge between project teams and business stakeholders. The practice should define both product and project requirements as well as related functional and nonfunctional requirements. Requirements definition should begin early in the analysis phase." [28]

Responsible/Accountable/Consulted/Informed (RACI) – "describes the roles of those involved in" activities. "It describes stakeholders as having one or more of the following responsibilities for a given task or deliverable:

[R]esponsible - does the work,

[A]ccountable - is the decision maker (only one),

[C]onsulted - must be consulted prior to the work and gives input, and

[I]nformed - means that they must be notified of the outcome." [1]

Review and Analysis of Process Description and/or Diagram – a way of collecting data (or additional data) by reviewing and conducting further analysis on (e.g., existing process descriptions or diagrams, listing of intersections and dependencies, relevant project plans, strategic plans, implementation plans, or any documentation that can point to critical or limiting activities for this program; process description and/or diagram against the listing of chokepoints and bottlenecks that could degrade process's ability to fulfill the mission.)

Risk Analysis – "The process of identifying, estimating, and prioritizing risks to organizational operations (including mission, functions, image, reputation), organizational assets, individuals, other organizations, and the Nation, resulting from the operation of an information system.

Part of risk management incorporates threat and vulnerability analyses, and considers mitigations provided by security controls planned or in place.". [NIST SP 800-39] and [NISTIR 8062]

Root Cause Analysis – "a structured examination of an identified problem to understand the underlying causes." [1]

Scenario – "an analysis model that describes a series of actions or tasks that respond to an event.

Each scenario is an instance of a use case." [1]

Scope Modeling – "used to define the scope of the analysis or the scope of the solution." [1]

Sensitivity/Uncertainty Analysis – "process of recalculating outcomes under alternative assumptions to determine the impact of a variable." [32]

Sequence Diagrams – "type of diagram that shows objects participating in interactions and the messages exchanged between them." [1]

Survey – "administers a set of written questions to stakeholders in order to collect responses from a large group in a relatively short period of time." [1]

Systems Analysis – "the act, process, or profession of studying an activity (such as a procedure, a business, or a physiological function) typically by mathematical means in order to define its goals or purposes and to discover operations and procedures for accomplishing them most efficiently." [20]

Use Case – "an analysis model that describes the tasks that the system will perform for actors and the goals that the system achieves for those actors along the way." [1]

Visualization – "1: formation of mental visual images; or 2: the act or process of interpreting in visual terms or of putting into visible form." [20]

Workflow Analysis – "entails reviewing all processes in an organization with a view toward identifying inefficiencies and recommending improvements." [29]

Appendix D—Illustrative Examples of Using Criticality Analysis Process Model

D.1 Example A – Enterprise Resource Planning (ERP) System Design

Exposition/Situation

An organization is replacing the asset management portion of their Enterprise Resource Planning (ERP) system. The new system will process a variety of data including potentially sensitive personnel and mission data. It will connect to other portions of the ERP system, including human resources, acquisition/supply chain, and finance applications. The system will consist of a mixture of custom-built and COTS hardware and software components.

The organization does not have a set of standardized security requirements for acquisition. Criticality levels for systems and components have not been established. A FIPS 199 Impact Level for the system has been established.

Due to the complexity of the project and the potential risk involved, the Project Manager decides to use the Criticality Analysis Process Model to prioritize different subsystems, components, and subcomponents within the system to ensure that appropriate levels of care are applied to those subsystems, components, and subcomponents.

Action

Process A – Criticality Analysis Procedure Definition

The Project Manager reviews the organization's strategic plan, risk management plan, and other documentation and determines that the organization does not have any formal criticality analysis procedures. The Project Manager does not have the authority nor the time and ability to perform a criticality analysis of the entire organization, which would be ideal. However, it is early enough in the ERP project that an analysis can be written into the project plan prior to and concordant with system procurement and implementation.

A.1 The Project Manager delegates to an employee with business analysis training, the process of integrating criticality analysis activities into the project plan. The Business Analyst[9] uses the Criticality Analysis Process Model in this publication to determine appropriate tasks, roles, and responsibilities based on Processes B, C, D, and E of the Model. The Project Manager and Business Analyst coordinate with a legal representative to identify laws, regulations, and organizational policies which may impact the project; they discuss with the rest of the project team how the criticality analysis may align with or impact their normal activities and discuss ways to address any concerns they have. The Business Analyst works with the project team to compare the guidance in the *Related Processes Outside of Criticality Analysis* in each Process and Sub-process description

---

[9]In the context of this document, any role mentioned, such as "Business Analyst," is not a specific title but a role of a person engaged in the program.

with the organization's existing processes to ensure that security engineering and risk management processes are appropriately integrated and planned for.

Once the Business Analyst and Project Manager determine they have designed a process that is appropriately integrated into their project plan, they meet with the rest of the project team along with others who will be participating in the criticality analysis to review and finalize the process. The plan they have designed follows the process defined in this document, with the addition of organizational-specific policies and procedures mentioned.

Process B - Conduct Program-Level Criticality Analysis

Once the project begins, the Project Manager ensures that procedures for conducting a criticality analysis have been adequately defined and are appropriate to be used for this system integration effort. Although there have been a few changes to the project plan, none impact the criticality analysis procedure defined in Process A. The Project Manager checks with the individual responsible for the broader ERP system and individuals responsible for the programs which the system will support – mostly inventory managers - to see if Criticality Levels have been assigned to those systems/programs or the information they process/store/transmit. Although some information is labeled as sensitive to the organization (i.e. "controlled unclassified information"), criticality or priority levels have not been defined. The Project Manager works with the inventory managers to execute Process B, with the help of the Business Analyst, a legal representative, the chief ERP program manager, and others when necessary.

B.1 As part of the project planning process, the Project Manager works with relevant stakeholders to define assumptions about the project, including the expected budget and timeline. He also defines how much detail is needed regarding goals and assumptions of the project to ensure that those are usable and appropriately inform the overall system development. Within the scope defined, the Project, ERP, and Inventory Managers collect documentation that contains organizational and program goals and objectives, such as the organizational strategic plan, mission and vision statement, shareholder reports, program board reviews, and management goals. They also identify relevant security, safety, privacy, and industry-specific laws and regulations [e.g., Federal Information Security Management Act (FISMA), North American Electric Reliability Corporation (NERC) Critical Infrastructure Protection (CIP), Federal Financial Institutions Examination Council (FFIEC) IT Handbook]. They define several program goals related to information security and safety that were not already documented.

B.2 The Project Manager uses the information from B.1 to develop a high-level description for how the inventory and ERP program goals and objectives are currently accomplished and how this will change with the new system. The Project Manager interviews senior managers to determine why they decided to implement a new system – their main concern was that the current system was outdated and did not allow real-time information sharing between organizational units and suppliers.

The Program Manager delegates to a Business Analyst the task of developing a representation of processes. The Business Analyst interviews several personnel responsible for inventory management on how they perform their duties and how they expect to use the system, including what they would like the system to do which is not possible with the existing process. This person conducts brainstorming discussions with relevant personnel, asking the following questions (among others):

- What information and tools do you use? Where do they come from? Is that information sensitive or does it have an impact/risk categorization associated with it?
- What information or tools would you require to perform the bare minimum necessary, such as during a severe weather event, even at a reduced speed or quality?
- What information, tools, or other products do you create? Where do they go?
- What is the biggest roadblock you face in performing your tasks?
- How long can a process be delayed before the organization is noticeably affected?
- Which processes must be completed before another process begins?
- How do you know when a process you depend on is completed, or the information/tool you need is available?
- How do you know that information you rely on is correct or tools you use are operating correctly?
- What organizational unit(s) or personnel do you work most closely with?

The Business Analyst uses the gathered information to develop a draft, high-level visual mapping of an updated inventory management process. This information will also be used in developing design requirements for the new system.

B.3 The Business Analyst analyzes the interactions, intersections, connections, and dependencies within the high-level visual mapping developed in B.2. Four main workflows in the inventory management process are identifiable – one for costly technological equipment (e.g., servers), one for costly, non-technological assets (e.g., real estate), one for raw materials used in products, and one for changes to equipment (e.g., change in location, project, owner). Several chokepoints in the process are highlighted.

The Business Analyst reviews this information with the Project Manager who compares the information with the goals defined in B.1. With this information, the Project Manager identifies areas where the new inventory management system may help the existing process better align with organizational goals. He updates the visual mapping created in B.2 to include details related to the flow of information, show the workflow paths, and highlight concerns. The Business Analyst reviews the updated process map with the inventory management personnel to validate it, address any concerns they have, and obtain their buy-in regarding any changes to their existing processes.

B.4 The Business Analyst conducts further interviews and brainstorming sessions with key personnel in the inventory management process along with representatives from the legal, safety, security, privacy, and acquisition departments to discuss how the planned workflow is expected to operate under both normal and abnormal conditions. The Business Analyst broadly scopes the discussion to the four identified workflow paths. The following questions (among others) are used to help the discussion:

- What other processes within a workflow will be impacted if one of the processes is compromised?
- Which organizational goals and objectives will be directly affected if a workflow output is compromised?
- How much of a delay in a workflow path can occur before other processes are impacted?

The Business Analyst then narrows the discussion to individual processes or activities within the workflow paths. Using the mapping developed in B.3, the Business Analyst uses the following questions to help guide the discussion:

- What might happen to the process if an input (e.g., information) is received early?
- What might happen to the process if an input is received late?
- What might happen to the process if an input received is noticeably incorrect or missing something?
- What might happen to the process if an input received is functional or has all required pieces but also has additional, unexpected pieces (e.g., extra, information that have not been requested)?
- How might a delay or compromise in one process impact the overall goals of the program (including safety, privacy, and security goals)?
- How might a problem in the process (e.g., delay, compromise of information, corruption of information, privacy problems for individuals) be identified?

B.5 Next, the Business Analyst and Project Manager use this information to rank or prioritize each of the process workflow paths from most important to least important by how vital they are to the success of the goals and objectives defined in B.1, applicable laws and regulations, and how strongly an adverse operating state will affect the program goals and objectives. They initially rank each process or activity defined in the process map in an ordinal list, but with more deliberation, decide to group the list into categories of "highly critical," "moderately critical," and "less critical," which becomes the Baseline Criticality of those activities. By comparing the criticality levels of each process, the Project Manager can rank the associated workflow paths.

Process C

With the project goals and assumptions defined and program-level Baseline Criticality Levels completed, the Project Manager decides to hire a company to help with the system design process; the project then moves to the system design phase. This portion of the criticality analysis is delegated to the contractor in charge of systems architecture (the Lead Systems Architect). She reviews the artifacts produced so far with the Project Manager.

C.1 The Lead Systems Architect and Project Manager start by defining how the system being designed will support the workflow paths that were defined in Process B. Because the scope of the criticality analysis is already limited by the scope of the project to a single system (the inventory management system), they decide to make the analysis more detailed and scope the analysis to only those subsystems that support activities and workflow paths that have been designated "highly critical" in Process B. The Lead Systems Architect collects and reviews the relevant artifacts of Process B, plus more detailed documentation of the existing inventory management and ERP systems that was not included in Process B, including backup plans, the FIPS 199 impact level for the system, and relevant High Value Asset (HVA) designations. She also reviews other documentation describing the existing infrastructure, including the network topology, power requirements, etc.

C.2 Early in the system design process, using documentation gathered in Process C.1 along with the map and interview results from Process B, the Lead Systems Architect works with the Project

Manager and the team of engineers to identify functionalities and capabilities needed to support the critical processes identified in Process B. She identifies existing subsystems – hardware, software, procedures, personnel, or other tools - which may be used to provide those functionalities and capabilities. She includes existing subsystems meant to protect or monitor those subsystems (i.e., controls). She identifies those functionalities and capabilities which will require a subsystem to be developed, modified, or purchased.

C.3 Once the Lead Engineer has roughly defined all functions required for the new system and developed a draft system diagram as part of the project design process, she and her team identify interactions, intersections, connections, and dependencies between the subsystems, focusing on identifying any subsystem outside the scope of the project with which a subsystem interacts, especially in the ERP system. Their review questions may include:

- Where do inputs to a critical process come from?
- Where do the outputs of a critical process go?
- What information/data is processed? Is that information/data sensitive or categorized? Are there special handling requirements associated with the information/data?
- What is required for providing the output in a timely, accurate, and complete manner?
- Which subsystem processes must be completed before the next process takes over?
- What subsystems/functions/processes are used to ensure that the subsystems perform their roles as required?
- What subsystems/functions/processes interact with or connect to a critical subsystem?

Using this information, they identify those subsystems and functions which directly perform or support a highly critical process, those which indirectly support a highly critical process, and those which are immaterial to the critical process. The Lead Systems Architect uses this information to modify the draft system diagram developed in C.2 slightly and to highlight key areas of importance.

C.4 The Lead Systems Architect works with her team of engineers to document generally the characteristics of each subsystem and how the subsystems should function when operating normally. They then analyze how each subsystem will behave under the following conditions:

- A subsystem is given an incomplete input;
- A subsystem is given an incorrect input;
- A subsystem is given an input at the wrong time or slowly;
- An IT/OT subsystem is not given enough power or too much power;
- An IT/OT subsystem is given a software/firmware update.

They validate their analysis by brainstorming certain scenarios and how the system will be impacted. They consider situations such as:

- An incorrectly applied patch;
- A zero-day vulnerability is discovered in a critical subsystem;
- Individuals object to operation of the system due to privacy problems arising from the processing of data
- A subsystem spontaneously produces abnormal outputs;

- A key person resigns;
- A subsystem is no longer supported by a vendor; and
- Adverse weather or other situations violate predefined conditions (e.g., excess heat, flooding, or power surges).

This information helps the engineers to identify areas where additional controls are needed to protect the system. They modify the system design multiple times to include appropriate security, safety, privacy and other controls and to incorporate different types of subsystems, then repeat the analysis. In the analysis, the engineers view each control as if it were a subsystem. For example, the engineers consider the value of using a distributed or a centralized database based on the organization's confidentiality, integrity, and availability needs. The Lead Systems Architect documents the results of this analysis in a series of descriptions of operating states.

C.5 Using this information, the Lead Systems Architect works with the Project Manager to rank the subsystems (including controls) from most important to least important. They ask the following questions (among others):

- What will happen to the system functions and operations if a subsystem's operating state is abnormal?
- How many connected or related subsystems would be impacted?
- Which of the subsystems are absolutely necessary for the system to operate, even at a reduced state or slower speed?

The Lead Systems Architect then decides on the thresholds for grouping the subsystems into High, Moderate, and Low, which become the Baseline Criticality levels of each subsystem. She validates all the information garnered from this process with the Project Manager, who in turn reviews it with the ERP Program Manager to ensure consistency and to identify any potential concerns.

Process D

Based on the Baseline Criticality Levels for the subsystems, the Program Manager and Lead Engineer narrow the scope of the criticality analysis to the most critical subsystems. For the purposes of this example, two subsystems were identified for further analysis: the inventory database and the in-house application used to access and modify that database. The Lead Engineer reviews the artifacts produced so far with the Program Manager.

D.1 The Lead Systems Engineer starts with identifying those subsystems that were assigned High Baseline Criticality Level in Process C: the inventory database which is stored with a cloud service provider, and a software application which has yet to be developed. The analysis for the database is led by the Project Manager as it deals with a third-party service provider's equipment and security controls; the analysis of the application is delegated to the System Engineer in charge of the application. He reviews the artifacts of Processes B and C and discusses with a legal representative relevant laws and regulations to help provide additional information about any requirements for components and subcomponents. For each analysis, the Program Manager defines, with input from the legal representative and Lead System Engineer, the level of detail that is necessary and possible for the analysis.

D.2 The Project Manager and Lead Engineer begin the process of identifying which third-party service provider they will use for hosting the inventory database, based on input from Process C. They request any documentation available related to the design of the service, including security, privacy, and availability features and how the provider will assure that the project's needs are met.

The System Engineer for the software application requests any documentation available related to the design of the application, including a description of relevant processes, functions, policies, and constraints (e.g., organization-specific security requirements, types of equipment used to access the application, etc.). Using this information, the systems engineer and his team create a preliminary listing of major functionalities and capabilities that will be performed by the subsystem. Because the System Engineer's team will be using an agile method to develop the software application, they will use this analysis to frame their initial scope of work.

D.3 The system engineers identify interactions, intersections, connections, and dependencies within the software application, including non-software components such as user input and behavior. The following questions are used but not limited to:

- Which components accept data inputs, process and/or store that data, and present the data when requested as an output? What is the sensitivity level or categorization of that data?
- What inputs are required for the subsystem to function as expected (timely, accurate, and complete)?
- Who or what provides those inputs?
- Which component must be operational or completed before another can begin?
- What software language(s), software libraries, or other components will be used?
- How will updates, upgrades, and other changes to components impact the subsystem?

The system engineers develop rough wireframes and flowcharts to express this information, then validates it with the lead engineer.

D.4 The systems engineers, working with security and privacy engineers, document how each component of the subsystem will function when operating normally and abnormally. The following situations are considered but not limited to:

- Insufficient power;
- Data overload;
- Incorrect data input;
- Operation in extreme temperatures;
- Failed or malfunctioning microchip component;
- Unsuccessful or erroneous firmware update; and
- Unexpected shortage of subcomponents.

System engineers document results of each of their analyses in a series of descriptions of operating states.

The Project Manager reviews the third-party cloud provider documentation to identify how the various components of their service will operate in both normal and adverse situations, and how it will impact the database. System engineers develop a high-level description of operating states focusing on the loss of confidentiality, integrity, and/or availability of the database.

D.5 Both groups work with their relevant stakeholders to assign Baseline Criticality levels to components using the information developed in D.2 to D.5. The following questions are used but not limited to:

- What will happen to the functions/capabilities delivered by the subsystem when components or subcomponents fail, resulting in an adverse operating state?
- What will be the impact to subsystem operations?
- Which of the components are most important for the subsystem to continue operating, even at a reduced state or slower speed?

The system engineer ranks the components of the software application (including non-software components such as user behavior) from most important to least important. They use this information to determine what functions to prioritize in the development process and which may be left to later. They then decide on the thresholds grouping the components into High, Moderate, and Low groups, which become the Baseline Criticality levels for each component.

D.1-5 (multiple iterations) Because the development of the software application is following an agile methodology, they repeat the criticality analysis in parallel with the development of the application. D.1 and D.2 are used to help scope the tasks and identify the functions which will be developed or improved and are conducted during sprint planning meetings; D.3 is completed during the sprint as part of documentation; D.4 and D.5 are done during the testing and evaluation portions of the sprint. In a few cases, the systems engineers decided to do an additional, more detailed iteration of the analysis to identify critical subcomponents of highly critical components. This was done, for example, with the user interface, and helped identify user inputs that might exploit a vulnerability resulting in an impact to the integrity or availability of the database.

Process E

With Baseline Criticalities assigned across the program activities/workflow paths, subsystems of the system under development, and components/subcomponents, the Project Manager, Lead Systems Architect, Lead Systems Engineer, and lead security engineer and privacy engineer begin to review baseline criticalities for consistency, interdependencies, and to develop final subsystem and component/subcomponent criticality levels. They also include the ERP program manager in this analysis as the system is closely connected to and tied with others under the ERP system umbrella.

E.1 Those persons responsible for conducting processes B, C, and D, meet to review the artifacts and results from their respective processes. They identify connection points where data or information will flow between components, any components across the different subsystems which are very similar in functionality, which components or component types will be used to support more than one subsystem, groups of components supplied by the same manufacturer, and finally groups of components expected to fail around the same time frame. The group performs this same analysis for the subsystems, identifying connections, commonalities, and repetitions. The tracing of components all the way through the program activities and workflows helps to identify any interdependencies that have not been considered in the analysis up to this point. The group documents result of this analysis using diagrams of interdependencies. They determine that there was a set of interdependencies and duplications across the inventory management system and the broader ERP system related to modifying inventory information.

E.2 The group then identifies what existing controls have been designated to monitor and protect the system, subsystems, and components. These controls include traditional security controls such as access control, configuration management, secure design principles, network and system activity monitoring functions, software switches, etc., as well as privacy controls such as notices, de-identification measures, privacy-enhancing cryptographic protocols, data tags, privacy-protective sensor configurations, etc.; they may be automated, technical, or manual. These controls can be documented in a variety of places, including security and privacy requirements, security and privacy plans, risk treatment plans, etc. The group determines that some controls included in the design may be excessive and that no control existed to prevent a resource shortage with regards to the interdependencies identified in E.1. The engineers responsible for those components modify their design slightly to compensate and the group reanalyzes the impact of the operating states of the components and controls.

E.3 The group then traces the impact of operating states that were defined in B.4, C.4, and D.4 to determine what adverse operating states may have a cascading effect across the subsystems, system, and project processes. The group reviews the controls in place at each level and what would happen to the program if the control(s) entered an adverse operating state. The group finds that a failure in one portion of the software application could lead to a cascading failure of the broader ERP system.

E.4 Next, the group reviews available security and privacy risk documentation to see if components/subcomponents, the subsystems, or the system itself should be assigned a higher criticality level than what has been assigned during the process thus far. Using existing risk assessment, threat assessment, impact analysis, or any similar documentation, the group evaluates the controls identified in E.2, the impact of operating states on those controls in E.3, and the Baseline Criticality Levels assigned in processes B, C, and D. It was determined that some of the components originally designated as lower criticality were connected to portions of the ERP system which, if an incorrect input was provided, would have significant impact. The criticality levels of these components were increased. The criticality levels of controls which may protect against such an event were also increased.

E.5 Finally, the group reviews analysis results from Process E to determine how Baseline Criticality Levels that were assigned to the system, its subsystems, and components/subcomponents should be revised to assign final Criticality Levels. This analysis considers identified interdependencies, controls, and any aspects of the system, subsystem, and component/subcomponent operations that may be vulnerable due to systems architecture and design, reliance on a single supplier, or any other factors that were discovered in the overall analysis.

Once Criticality Levels have been finalized, the program manager distributes the results to the groups performing risk analysis, threat analysis, impact analysis, contingency planning, and systems engineering activities. Criticality Levels are then used to inform these activities and help refine how they are planned and performed in the future. Criticality Levels also provide valuable inputs into the design and refinement of security requirements and controls, help shape system and component (hardware and software) testing, determine if any components should be bought in advance and stockpiled, and to inform supplier diversification decisions.

Later, Criticality Levels are used to inform future system development and integration efforts, as well as future procurements and modernization efforts.

D.2   Example B – SmartCity Concept Development

An organization is considering developing a plot of land encompassing about 200 acres. The CEO of the organization would like to use the land to create a futuristic "smart city" (called "Smartstown, USA"). Because there is a lot of talk about privacy and cybersecurity, the CEO wants Smartstown, USA, to be safe, secure, and attractive to both businesses and residents. The organization is concerned that such a goal is unreasonable, and that this large and innovative project has a high likelihood of failure. They have spoken with many subject matter experts, both inside and outside of the organization, and found that there is little consensus regarding an approach to take; each expert views their area of expertise as being critical to the success of the project and experts are unwilling to compromise. The organization decides to conduct a high-level criticality analysis to identify key areas of risk, which they can then focus on in more depth.

Process A

The organization develops a working group to brainstorm the project at a high level. This group consists of experienced urban planners as well as legal, technology, and health/safety representatives. None of the players have conducted a criticality analysis before, but some have conducted similar analyses such as project risk analyses, business process analyses, and failure/hazard analyses.

A.1 The group reviews the criticality analysis process in this publication and tailors it to their own purposes. They define rules of behavior and a time limit for the analysis. Since much is unknown at this point, they decide that the scope, method of analysis, and participants will be defined separately at the beginning of each Process (Processes B, C, D, and E). They determine that the scope of the analysis will be limited to a thought exercise, meaning they will not commit to any specific technologies or solutions at this point. Once the project begins in earnest, they will review and revise the analysis to include specific solutions.

Process B

The group decides to perform most of Process B in a two-day workshop with all the working group participants.

B.1 Prior to the workshop, the working group develops a high-level scope for the analysis based on input from the CEO and other key stakeholders. The plan will include commercial, living, civic, and recreational spaces. The smart city concept will utilize different types of electronic data collection sensors to help manage resources. The group will consider emerging trends such as driverless vehicles, modular building structures, automated utility management and control, alternative energy sources, electric vehicles, a large number of interconnected/Internet of Things (IoT) devices, next-generation optical fibers, high-tech waste management solutions, and other relevant trends.

The group gathers any relevant documents that they feel they may need.

They decide to modify the model described in this publication by combining processes B.2 and B.3.

B.2/B.3 During the workshop, the group brainstorms a list of everything they would like the city to have. They separate into groups to run through scenarios of the types of lives people might live in Smartstown, detailing what they would need to be happy. For example, a family with three children would need easy access to day care, schools, school buses or other transportation, grocery stores, clothing outlets, sporting good outlets, after-school activities, dental, medical, urgent care, and emergency services. The groups review surveys and research conducted on what people want in their neighborhoods. For example, they find that residents with children place an emphasis on safety, quality school systems/day care, and a place where children can safely go without the parents. They review their list and visually link the resources. They find that all the resources rely on access to transportation.

The workshop participants create a set of workflow paths for each scenario showing what the residents do on a typical weekday, a typical weekend, on a holiday, and if something bad happens. For example, one workflow path for the family of three may look like this:

- Wake up, get dressed, etc.
- Prepare and eat breakfast
- Oldest child walks to school
- Middle child catches school bus
- Youngest child taken to day care
- Parents go to work
- Parents meet for lunch
- Oldest child goes to after-school activity
- Middle child goes to after-school activity
- Parent picks up youngest child and drives to pick up oldest child
- All meet at middle child's after school activity
- All go home
- Prepare and eat dinner
- Children do homework and go to bed
- Parents watch television and go to bed

The group decides to develop separate workflow paths describing events if one of the children becomes injured and in the event of adverse weather (e.g., snowstorm or hurricane).

The workshop participants get back together and compare the scenarios they have developed. They review how the scenarios intersect by asking the question: "At what point might these people cross paths?" They group activities into categories: travel, work, school, eating, shopping, recreation, medical/dental, and home-life. The participants find that each scenario includes a significant amount of traveling, either using public transportation, walking, or driving. During this review period, some of the groups add or modify their scenarios slightly to include things they forgot or wanted to express differently.

B.4 On the second day of the workshop, the group again separates into sub-groups and begins defining operating states. They review each activity and how the rest of the scenario would be impacted if that activity: (1) did not happen, (2) happened slower than it should, (3) happened in an unsafe, insecure or privacy-invasive manner, (4) happened quicker than normal, and (5) happened on time but with an unexpected addition. At the same time, the groups rank the operating states in terms of severity for the scenario. For example, taking the youngest child to day care:

(1 - moderate) If the child is not taken to day care, the parents will have to take care of it. One of them will have to stay home from work or they will need to find a baby sitter.

(2 - moderate) If the child is late to day care, one of the parents may be late to work and as a result, may be late leaving work. Also, the day care provider may limit the number of times a child can be late which may eventually result in the parents needing to find a new day care provider or pay a fine to the current day care for late pickup.

(3 - high) If the child is taken to day care in an unsafe manner (for example, by a parent who is driving recklessly or the child is not properly restrained in its seat), the child may be seriously injured. For this example, the group developed a scenario where the child arrives at the day care provider with signs of whiplash. The day care provider recognizes the child is injured and calls emergency services. The child is taken by ambulance to the hospital, child protective services arrives to investigate, the parents leave work to go to the hospital, and they arrange for transportation and childcare for the other two children. Privacy as a concern was brought up at this time. The group discussed what information related to this situation may represent a privacy risk, for example the child's healthcare records, any camera recordings of the event, and any paper or digital recording of any legal action taken.

(4 - low) If the child arrives at day care early, the facility may not be open yet and so the parent and child must wait in the parking lot until they open.

(5 – moderate to high) For this example, the group devised a scenario where the child arrives at day care as planned, but is carrying a germ. The other children and adults in the day care may catch the germ. If it is something like norovirus, the day care may be shut down for a few days and will need to be sanitized.

B.5 Once operating states are defined for each activity in each scenario, the groups meet again to review the results of their analysis. They use the same categories as before and use sticky-notes to put up the severity rankings developed in B.4. They roughly develop histograms of the severity rankings for each category and discuss them. As a group, they create baseline criticality levels for each category. (This is modified from the model described in this publication which recommends developing criticality levels for each workflow path. This shows one way the model may be adapted.)

It is found that there are a lot of similarities in the operating states for the activities related to travel. Although the scenarios generally ranked the adverse operating states of travel-related activities as "moderate," because of the number of activities relying on travel, the group decided to give the travel category an overall baseline criticality ranking of "high." Medical/dental was also ranked "high" as many scenarios identified adverse operating states related to injury/illness and rated them between moderate and high.

Process C

Using the information garnered from Process C, the organization conducts system-level analyses. They decide that they will be performing at least two system-level analyses: one for the transportation infrastructure, and one for the medical/dental infrastructure. This example will focus on the transportation infrastructure.

C-1 The organization develops working groups for each analysis. The transportation working group is composed of urban planners, legal representatives, transportation experts, automotive vehicle researchers, and others. Each workshop agrees to a set of rules. They set a time limit of ½ day for their analyses. Prior to the workshop, the participants are given information from Process B to review.

C-2 The working group reviews the scenarios developed in Process B. They brainstorm a list of every transportation-related function and capability needed to support those scenarios. To help with this process, they ask the questions "Who uses the infrastructure?" and "How is it used?" They use both the information from Process B as well as their own expert knowledge to answer this question.

They decide that the roads should allow for smooth flow of traffic allowing residents a predictable travel time. There must be infrastructure in place to support newer vehicle types such as electric, hybrid, and autonomous vehicles. The group decides to plan for the increased use of delivery services and to ensure that delivery vehicles do not obstruct traffic. Public transportation is heavily used in the nearby metropolitan area, and so the group decides to support commuters who wish to travel to the metropolitan area by providing connecting public transportation services. During this brainstorming exercise, the group roughly prioritizes the functions and criticalities listed.

C-3 The group begins identifying what types of systems might be used to support the functions and requirements defined in C-2. This process often results in the identification of additional requirements and functions. They list things such as roads, crosswalks/bridges, gas stations, electric vehicle charging stations, signage and painting that support automated vehicles, the vehicles themselves, and the communications systems that allow vehicles to communicate with other systems (e.g., GPS). They also identify the means to clean the streets and drains to ensure that the signage and painting remain visible, accessible transportation stations, reliable and fast train or similar system, reliable bus or tram system, school bus or other transport, support for taxi or other service, parking (public, delivery, bus, repair, long-term, etc.), bicycle and pedestrian paths/lanes, etc. They identify some technologies that are futuristic and bring in experts to identify what sort of things those technologies will need to operate to expand their list.

C-4 The group loosely defines a set of rules for each function/requirement by which one could tell that the system is operating at peak efficiency. For example, the drive time between point X and point Y will be 30 to 35 minutes. The group then loosely defines adverse operating states for each function and requirement defined. They also roughly assign significance levels for the operating states. For example, in the case GPS functionality:

> (1-Low) If GPS does not work in the area, drivers may be unable to reach their destinations and may create congestion as they drive around trying to find places.

> (2-Low-Moderate) If GPS works sporadically or slowly in the area, it may distract or cause drivers to miss a turn, which may cause them to swerve and potentially cause an accident.

> (3-Moderate-High) If GPS in the area is compromised, it could result in the theft of personally identifiable information (PII) and potentially the modification of GPS data, and aggregation of travel points could permit the tracking of persons (including high-profile persons and

children) and could reveal sensitive information, including health information, religious activity, and other personal habits.

(4-Low) GPS operating more efficiently than needed would waste resources.

(5-Low) If GPS in the area has extraneous information, it could cause confusion.

C-5 The group reviews the operation states of each function/requirement and ranks them in terms of impact. The group finds that communications between vehicles and the transportation infrastructure is by far the most impactful element, whether it is the drivers reading road signs or autonomous vehicles registering an approaching emergency vehicle.

Process D

The organization decides to narrow the analysis further to identify critical components of the system. They tailor this analysis to their organization and to the scope of the analysis. They perform step D-4 prior to step D-3 (for this example, the steps are numbered as in the model, but are rearranged). A group is formed consisting of experts in the fields of transportation, including urban planners, automated vehicle researchers, network and vehicle designers/engineers, and cybersecurity and privacy professionals.

D-1 Because the analysis is limited in scope to theoretical applications without identifying any specific technology solutions, the working group cannot conduct a thorough analysis of risks in this area. Non-electronic communication was determined to be out of scope for this analysis. They decide to have a one-day workshop to collect what they can from a high-level perspective.

D-2 The group begins by identifying all the components that are involved in the concept of communicating between a vehicle and the infrastructure. They list things such as: the car itself; the driver; the sensors in a car used to aid the driver; the mechanisms in an automated vehicle used to process data from sensors; the mechanisms in an automated vehicle to translate that data into commands which the car will follow; and the electronic communication between the vehicle and the infrastructure. (e.g., GPS communications or if a stop light notifies cars in the area that it is turning red. Non-electronic communication is out of scope for this example.)

The group reviews the components listed and identifies how each of them are connected. In some cases, additional components are included. The group finds that there are several workflow paths depending on the communication origin, but that all the workflow paths use the same set of processes to register and interpret the communication.

D-4 The group defines operating states for each component type. For example, for a sensor:

(1-Moderate-High) If a sensor does not function, the vehicle will not register a warning such as an approaching obstacle and may cause an accident.

(2-Moderate-High) If a sensor is slow, it may have the same results as if it didn't operate at all.

(3-High) If a sensor operates erratically or is compromised, it may register an obstacle when there isn't one and cause an accident.

(4-Moderate) If a sensor operates overly efficiently, potentially collecting additional information or information in greater detail than was anticipated, privacy problems may arise.

(5-High) If a sensor operates as expected, but has an added feature which allows a malicious entity to view the information the sensor collects, it could represent a significant privacy concern.

D-3 The group decides that, because of the scope of this analysis, they cannot reasonably identify the individual components which will be used. Instead, they list the types of components used, such as "sensor," "interpreter," "analyzer," and "operator." They create a system diagram showing the workflow paths as they move through each process and component type.

D-5 The group collects all the various operating states and scenarios to develop baseline criticality levels for the components. They decide that the sensors and the operator component types are the most critical as they had the most significant impact in this scope.

Process E

The organization collects all the information that was created in each of the component-level analyses. They find that, overall, there were five different components that were considered "critical." They chose to continue the analysis with these five components. Again, for this analysis, they chose to tailor the analysis to their needs.

E-1 The organization assigns representatives from each component-level analysis to meet with representatives from the system-level analysis. They will in turn meet with representatives from the process-level analysis. They set a time limit for this portion of the analysis.

E-2 The component-level teams review their analysis with the system-level and process-level representatives. For the communication component group, they review how sensors connect to and interact with other components in the system, and then other components of the smartcity, including those identified by the Medical/Dental working group (the other process besides transportation that was identified as highly critical). They find that sensors play a major role in the transportation system beyond the scope of their analysis. For example, sensors detecting congestion may activate a traffic response such as opening an additional lane, increasing tolls, or rerouting vehicles. The group brainstorms various controls at each level which may help prevent, detect, or respond to a problem. They review what might happen if the control fails and the likelihood of that happening.

E-3 The component-level teams review their operating states and scenarios with the rest of the group. They review how the controls identified in E-2 reduce the likelihood of the impact. In certain cases, they identify areas where they feel the baseline criticality levels don't represent the levels of impact or likelihood. For example, when comparing all the critical components, they find that the sensors which were identified as critical in the transportation process were also found to be critical in the medical/dental process because the emergency response vehicles are expected to communicate with the traffic signals and with automated vehicles to allow them safe and speedy passage. In addition, they use GPS and other communication technologies. It was found that most every process used a significant amount of wireless communication, and this might place a strain on the communications network.

E-4 The group has no threat, vulnerability, or other risk information to apply at this time. However, they identified a collection of resources to help them obtain this information. This included documents (e.g. NIST SP 800-30, NISTIR 8062), personnel (e.g. risk specialist), and organizations (e.g. the local InfraGard chapter).

E-5 The group reviews all the baseline criticality levels, along with their operating states and the potential controls which may be used. They alter several of the criticality levels to align with the priorities of safety, security, privacy, and residents' experience.

The organization uses this information to begin financing and designing their smart city concept. They approach the CEO with several design options and explain to him why certain decisions were made. They approach several potential builders and explain to them what their priorities are. The builders each have their own opinions on the matter and often the organization must reevaluate the criticality analysis to ensure that any changes to the design of the city are in alignment with the criticality analysis and the organization's priorities.

Appendix E—Criticality Analysis Process Model

Detailed version of high-level criticality process. Please note that this image is split into two parts for ease of printing. For alternate formats of the entire image, please see the Supplemental Content section of this publication.

Continued on next page

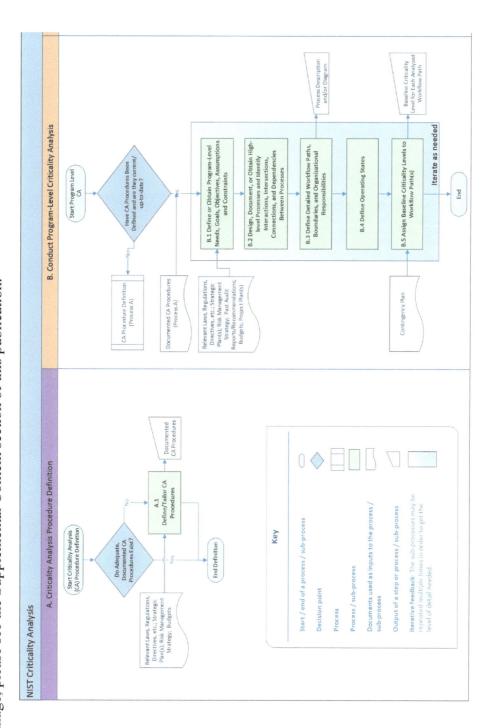

Figure 7 - NIST Criticality Analysis Process Model Part 1

CRITICALITY ANALYSIS PROCESS MODEL:
PRIORITIZING SYSTEMS AND COMPONENTS

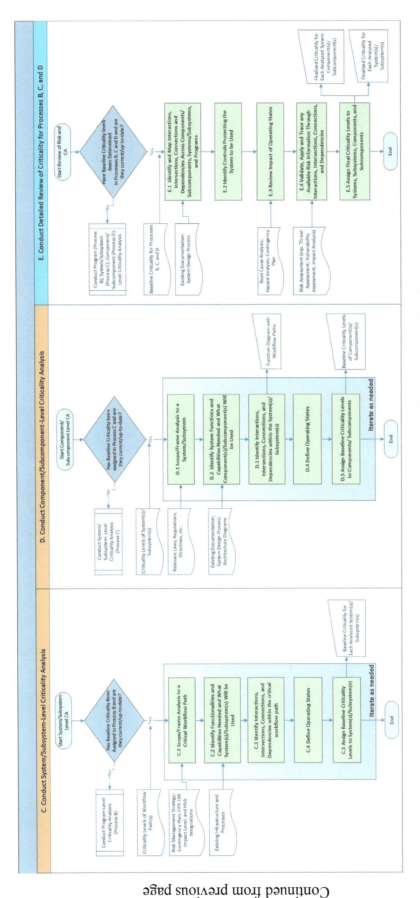

Figure 8 - NIST Criticality Analysis Process Model Part 2

www.ingramcontent.com/pod-product-compliance
Lightning Source LLC
Chambersburg PA
CBHW041420050326
40689CB00002B/589